JARROLD SHORT WALKS

for all the family

Cornwall

Compiled by
Sue Viccars

D0202260

JARROLD
publishing

Mapping sourced from   Ordnance Survey®

Dedication

For my Dad

Acknowledgements

With grateful thanks to all those who came and explored Cornwall with me, and especially to Jenny for constantly putting me up (and putting up with me!) and sharing the odd bottle of wine. Also to the National Trust Regional Office at Lanhydrock for so willingly supplying me with information.

Text:	Sue Viccars
Photography:	Sue Viccars
Editor:	Crawford Gillan
Designer:	Ellen Moorcraft

o⒮ Ordnance Survey® This product includes mapping data licensed from Ordnance Survey ® with the permission of the Controller of Her Majesty's Stationery Office. © Crown Copyright 2002. All rights reserved. Licence number 100017593. Pathfinder is a registered trade mark of Ordnance Survey, the national mapping agency of Great Britain.

ISBN 0-7117-2088-6

While every care has been taken to ensure the accuracy of the route directions, the publishers cannot accept responsibility for errors or omissions, or for changes in details given. The countryside is not static: hedges and fences can be removed, field boundaries can alter, footpaths can be rerouted and changes in ownership can result in the closure or diversion of some concessionary paths. Also, paths that are easy and pleasant for walking in fine conditions may become slippery, muddy and difficult in wet weather, while stepping-stones across rivers and streams may become impassable.

If you find an inaccuracy in either the text or maps, please write or e-mail Jarrold Publishing at one of the addresses below.

First published 2002
by Jarrold Publishing

Printed in Belgium
by Proost NV, Turnhout. 1/02

Jarrold Publishing
Pathfinder Guides, Whitefriars,
Norwich NR3 1TR
E-mail: pathfinder@jarrold.com
www.jarroldpublishing.co.uk/
pathfinders

Front cover: Port Quin
Previous page: The church of St Wynwallow, Landewednack

Contents

SCALE 1:277 777 or 1 INCH to about 4½ MILES *1CM to 2.7KM*

0   2   4   6   8   10   KILOMETRES   15

0   2   4   6   MILES   8   10

KEYMAP HEIGHTS SHOWN IN FEET

Keymap

7
18
20
South West Coast Path
Rumps Point
Pentire Point
Gunver Head
Trevose Head
Quies
Constantine Bay
Porthcothan
Park Head
Bedruthan Steps
Mawgan Porth
Berryl's Point
Watergate Bay
Vale of Mawgan or Lanherne
Towan Head
Fistral Bay
NEWQUAY
Kelsey Head
Holywell Bay
Penhale Point
Ligger or Perran Bay
Penhale Sands
Perranporth
Bawden Rocks or Man & his man
Goonhavern
PADSTOW
WADEBRIDGE
St Columb Major
St Breock Downs
Castle-an-Dinas
Indian Queens
Summercourt
St Enoder
Hensbarrow Downs
Grampound
Tintagel Head
Start Point
Port Isaac
Port Isaac Bay
Port Quin
Polzeath
Rock
St Merryn
St Eval
St Mawgan
Roche
Bugle
A39
A30
A392
A3058
A391
A390
A389
SCALE 1:277 777 or 1 INCH to about 4½ MILES 1CM to 2.7KM
0 2 4 6 8 10 KILOMETRES 15
0 2 4 6 MILES 8 10
KEYMAP HEIGHTS SHOWN IN FEET

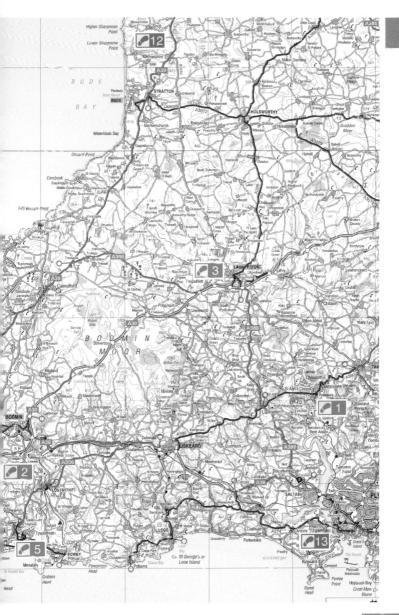

Introduction

For many, Cornwall is the ideal holiday destination. Characterful fishing villages; picturesque harbours; colourful local customs; sandy beaches; rugged cliffs; peaceful wooded estuaries; wild moorland; sunshine, ice creams and pasties. But just scratch beneath the surface and you will discover the real Cornwall, a land steeped in history and tradition with a remarkable industrial heritage

The Cornish people have a fierce sense of independence born of a physical remoteness from London, the traditional seat of power; of a centuries-long history of oppression and hardship; and of a unique social heritage. There is a wealth of prehistoric evidence here, from Neolithic chambered tombs and Bronze Age stone circles, to compact Iron Age villages and fortified cliff castles. The tradition of castle building continued, as at Tintagel, complete with tales of the legendary King Arthur; later, Henry VIII was responsible for the splendid castles overlooking the south-coast estuaries. Cornwall also has her fair share of fine houses: Lanhydrock is said to be one of the best examples of a late Victorian country house in Great Britain.

Life has always been hard here. Those involved in the traditional occupations – fishing, mining tin and copper, and small-scale farming – have adapted to shifting fortunes over the years. The mining industry has disappeared in the face of cheaper foreign imports; Cornwall is peppered with industrial memorabilia, such as the starkly beautiful engine houses. The demise of the fishing industry, only clinging in a few places, has meant that those settlements once reliant on fishing have had to adapt too. These villages now attract hundreds of holidaymakers each year, drawn by their picturesque settings and, increasingly, by the wealth of art and craft galleries. Cornwall has long been a mecca for artists, attracted by her natural beauty and superb light.

The county's equable climate has strongly influenced another of Cornwall's great attractions: her gardens. Sub-tropical plants flourish in the sheltered valleys of the south coast; snowdrops and daffodils bloom

Playing 'Pooh Sticks' on the River Fowey at Lanhydrock

earlier here than elsewhere on mainland Britain. The inspirational Eden Project, where visitors wander through space-age biomes containing incredible plants gleaned from all over the world, has already drawn hundreds of thousands of visitors; many have gone on to explore the area in more depth. Toursim forms a vital part of Cornwall's economy, assisted by improved transport links up country.

This book gives a taste of all Cornwall's attractions through a wide range of walks to suit all ages and abilities. Stroll around historic Launceston, 'the gateway to Cornwall'. Tackle a tough trek along cliffs of wild magnificence near Morwenstow, renowned not just for its natural power but for stories of smugglers and shipwrecks. Explore picturesque St Ives, once reliant on pilchard fishing, now setting for the Tate St Ives gallery. Wander along the wooded banks of the River Fal around the Trelissick estate, or explore the ruined coastal mine workings at Geevor, which – amazingly – only finally closed in 1990.

Cornwall is a beautiful, fascinating county, with superb natural scenery and a wonderful history, and has much to offer – and is best and most satisfactorily explored on foot!

1 *Cotehele*

START	Calstock
DISTANCE	3 miles (4.8km)
TIME	1½ hours
PARKING	Car park (free) in Calstock
ROUTE FEATURES	Fairly steep path up through woods from Cotehele Quay; dogs are not allowed within Cotehele garden

The historic village of Calstock, tucked away beside the tranquil River Tamar and now a mecca for local artists, provides a fitting start for a gentle riverside stroll which leads through woodland to beautiful Cotehele House, dating from the 15th/16th centuries, and its sympathetically restored quay, once a bustling port and lifeline for the Tamar valley.

From the car park walk downstream to pass the children's play area (left) and the Tamar Inn (right), towards the elegant concrete 12-arched viaduct, which was built from 1904–8 to carry the railway line from Calstock to Bere Alston. It's a magnificent sight, soaring 117½ ft (35.8m) above the river, and dwarfing the picturesque village of Calstock beneath. At the junction, turn left uphill, as if leaving the village.

The last working sailing barge on the **Tamar**, *Shamrock*, has been restored and can be seen at Lime Quay. Built in 1899, she is one of the country's last ketch-rigged sailing barges; she originally carried manure and traditional materials, and worked in the stone trade around Truro and Falmouth for many years. She is owned by the National Trust and the National Maritime Museum.

A Almost immediately, turn left along Lower Kelly, a narrow lane that runs along the edge of the river and passes

PUBLIC TRANSPORT Bus service from Callington, Gunnislake, Plymouth and Tavistock

REFRESHMENTS National Trust café and picnic area at Cotehele House and quay; Tamar Inn, Boot Inn and Riverside restaurant in Calstock

PUBLIC TOILETS By the car park in Calstock; at Cotehele

CHILDREN'S PLAY AREA By the car park in Calstock; at Cotehele

ORDNANCE SURVEY MAPS Explorer 108 (Lower Tamar Valley & Plymouth), Landranger 201 (Plymouth & Launceston)

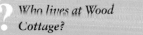

under the viaduct. Ahead and left you can catch glimpses of Cotehele House peering out from the trees. The lane passes Calstock boatyard on the left, and under an old bridge by a huge limekiln, then veers right up the Danescombe valley to pass the pottery.

> **? Who lives at Wood Cottage?**

B Where the track goes straight on, turn left following signs for Cotehele to enter woodland. The path climbs steeply; at the next fork keep right, signed Cotehele House. Look left to see the 15th-century domed dovecote; the path reaches the track that separates the house from the lower gardens. Turn left, then pass through a gate with the entrance to the house and gardens, with toilets, picnic area and 15th-century Barn Restaurant on the right.

C Walk into the car park and turn right. When you reach the

Cotehele is a most beautifully preserved and atmospheric Tudor house, built largely between 1485 and 1539 by the Edgcumbe family. Owned by the National Trust since 1947, Cotehele is still a working estate, in much the same way as it has been for more than 600 years, with market gardening, flower growing and small scale farming predominant. The varied gardens are superb all year round, and the valley garden that runs below the house downhill towards the Tamar provides an ideal location for a variety of tender and exotic species.

lane turn left downhill to 19th-century Cotehele Quay, with its beautifully restored warehouses and limekilns. The Higher (Lime) Quay was used for importing limestone (the oldest trade in the valley) to feed the kilns that can be seen all along the river, to produce calcium vital to correct the balance of the local acid soil; the Middle Quay brought in coal from South Wales; and the Lower Quay was used by paddle steamer passengers and for the export of the soft fruit and vegetables that were grown in the temperate climate of the Tamar valley. Silver, lead, copper and arsenic were also mined in the valley from as early as the 14th century, until the 19th century, and exported from quays such as Cotehele, and Morwellham, near Tavistock.

D Walk upriver to pass the Edgcumbe Arms café (a pub in the mid 19th century), and the gallery, on the left, and the car park and picnic area on the right, onto a level path, which hits a broader track running along the edge of the woodland. The path climbs a little to pass the Chapel in the Wood, dedicated to St George and St Thomas à Becket, and built by Sir Richard Edgcumbe in 1490 in gratitude for his escape from his enemies in 1483. Continue along the path to pass the Calstock viewpoint high above the river on the right, and to rejoin the outward route. Follow the path down through the woods; turn right by the pottery in Danescombe valley, then retrace your steps along the banks of the Tamar to Calstock and your car.

Calstock from Cotehele

Lanhydrock and the River Fowey

START Respryn Bridge

DISTANCE 2½ miles (4km) with possible 2½ mile (4km) extension

TIME 1 hour (plus 1 hour)

PARKING National Trust car park at Respryn Bridge (50p honesty box), signposted from B3268 Bodmin–Lostwithiel

ROUTE FEATURES No difficulties; dogs to be kept on a lead within Lanhydrock estate

2

Imposing late 19th-century Lanhydrock House and its magnificent estate provide the focus for this walk, which runs along the lovely River Fowey, explores the estate's beechwoods and farmland, then reaches the house itself, set in sweeping parkland. An optional (yet easy) extension to the route leads to Restormel Castle, 13th-century symbol of Norman authority.

This walk can easily be done in either direction, but taking it clockwise means that you might

Lanhydrock House and gardens provide a fascinating insight into late Victorian wealthy country life. Now in the care of the National Trust, Lanhydrock is one of the most impressive 19th-century houses in England. Only the original 17th-century gatehouse and north wing survived a terrible fire in 1881, the remainder of the house being rebuilt at that time. The beautiful gardens were also laid out in Victorian times.

arrive at Lanhydrock House in time for tea. Turn left out of the car park onto the lane, to cross the pretty five-arched Respryn Bridge, which dates from 1520.

A Over the bridge turn right to pass through a kissing gate, and

? *In what way did Spillers Foods help the Lanhydrock estate, and when? You will find the answer on a seat somewhere along the route.*

PUBLIC TRANSPORT Bus service from Bodmin (to Lanhydrock House)
REFRESHMENTS National Trust café at Lanhydrock House
PUBLIC TOILETS None on route; available inside Lanhydrock House
ORDNANCE SURVEY MAPS Explorer 107 (St Austell & Liskeard), Landranger 200 (Newquay & Bodmin)

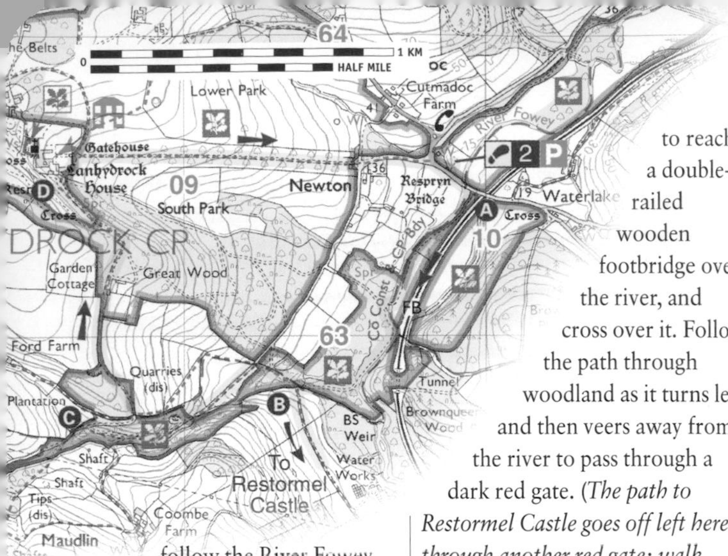

The map contains these labels:

Belts · 64 · 1 KM · HALF MILE · OC · Cutmadoc Farm · River Fowey · Lower Park · Gatehouse · Lanhydrock House · 09 · Newton · South Park · Respryn Bridge · 19 Waterlake · Cross · 10 · A · 2 P · DROCK CP · Garden Cottage · Great Wood · Sp · 63 · B · Coast · Co Bdy · Ford Farm · Quarries (dis) · B · C · Plantation · Tunnel · Brownqueen Wood · BS Weir · Shaft · To Restormel Castle · Water Works · Shaft · Tips (dis) · Coombe Farm · Maudlin · Shafts

follow the River Fowey downstream. The river, which has its source near Brown Willy, 1,375ft (419m) high up on Bodmin Moor, is quite lovely here, and particularly so in spring and autumn. Follow the wooded path

River Fowey below Respryn Bridge

to reach a double-railed wooden footbridge over the river, and cross over it. Follow the path through woodland as it turns left and then veers away from the river to pass through a dark red gate. (*The path to Restormel Castle goes off left here, through another red gate; walk across the fields to join a tarmac lane; where that lane veers right keep straight on along the farm lane to reach the castle, positioned on a high spur of land above the lane to the right.*) Walk on through the woods slightly uphill.

If you do feel like exploring a little farther, it's worth going to visit the imposing ruins of **Restormel Castle**, refurbished by Edmund, Earl of Cornwall (1272–99), in the 13th century. Restormel, the best preserved motte-and-bailey castle in the county, was probably Edmund's main residence and, with its surrounding deer park, became a forceful symbol of Norman power and prosperity.

B Where the track bends sharp right turn left, and walk along a

Lanhydrock's impressive gatehouse

level track with fields on the right and woodland on the left. As you enter Ford Plantation via two granite gateposts look out for the disused Jacob's quarry in the trees on the right. Stay on the track to meet another, where you turn sharp right under a huge oak tree.

C Follow the track through beech woodland steeply uphill. It runs through an open gateway, then along the edge of fields (with wonderful blackberries in September), and lovely views to the right over the wooded Fowey valley. The track passes through another dark red gate, then past Garden Cottage with its impressive walled garden (great hollyhocks in summer). Follow the gritty track on to pass through Lanhydrock's famous woodland garden, renowned for its camellias, rhododendrons and magnolias. The track ends at a wooden paling gateway.

D Go through the gate and turn right to walk past the entrance to the restaurant, toilets and church to the left, and along the outside of Lanhydrock House and formal gardens to reach the main gatehouse entrance. Turn right down The Avenue, flanked by a splendid double row of beech trees, to walk through glorious parkland to The Lodge; pass through the gates and walk straight on to meet the lane opposite Station Lodge. Turn right, and the National Trust car park will soon be found on the left. ●

3 *Launceston*

START Launceston	
DISTANCE 2 miles (3.2km)	
TIME 1 hour	
PARKING Long or short stay car parks (fee-paying) on Race Hill	
ROUTE FEATURES No difficulties	

The historic town of Launceston, walled in the 12th century and 'the gateway to Cornwall', is full of surprises, and there's something of interest for everyone on this easy walk which leads from the heart of the old town to run through peaceful fields, with great views to the Norman castle above, and returns via the steam railway, museum and 16th-century church.

Leave the car park and turn left up Race Hill. Take the first right (Bounsalls Lane), then immediately turn left up Windmill Lane (dead end). The lane ends at a turning area; walk ahead to enter Coronation Park, laid out as a pleasure gardens in 1895.

A Turn left along the tarmac path and walk downhill, passing the railed-off Windmill reservoir, completed in 1895, on the left. Little is known about the windmill from which the reservoir takes its name. Leave the park between the

> **?** *There is a memorial to Leonard Macleod Hender in Coronation Park. How, when and where did he die?*

children's play area and the leisure centre, to meet the road opposite Launceston College, and follow the road right. Pass Windmill Hill on the right; cross over Dunheved Road (note the original Launceston College building on the left; the school was founded by Wesleyan methodists in 1873) and turn left. Take the next right into Dunheved Fields, and the second right down

PUBLIC TRANSPORT Bus service from Bodmin, Bude, Exeter, Liskeard, Okehampton, Plymouth, Tavistock, Truro

REFRESHMENTS Wide range of pubs and cafés in Launceston

PUBLIC TOILETS In the car park

CHILDREN'S PLAY AREA In Coronation Park; in Tredyan Road

ORDNANCE SURVEY MAPS Explorer 112 (Launceston & Holsworthy), Landranger 201 (Plymouth & Launceston)

Hendra Vale. When Western Road is reached, cross over with care and go down Carboth Lane to reach Chapel.

The church of **St Mary Magdalene**, one of three in Launceston, is famed for its superbly carved exterior. The tower dates from 1380, and is the only feature remaining of the church built by Edward, the Black Prince. The present church was built by Henry Trecarrell in the early 16th century, to appease the souls of his ancestors when, tragically, he lost his family in 1511.

B Cross the lane, and follow footpath signs over a stile into a field. Turn left to cross another stile, then right. This is a lovely, gentle route along the bottom of the valley of Harpers Lake (stream) – a deer park in Norman times –

with great views of Launceston Castle opening up to the right. Cross another stile, then another to enter the final field, and through a five-bar gate onto a grassy track. Turn left, and over another stile, then on down the track and over another stile onto Wooda Lane, with allotments on the right, near the site of an old well – Maiden's Well.

C Turn left; follow the lane until it meets Tredyan Road; turn right to pass the children's playground on the right. Walk on to pass the steam railway on the left, a narrow-gauge line that runs along the Kensey valley as far as Newmills. Cross St Thomas Road (take care) and turn immediately right up steep St Thomas Hill. Cross Wooda Road at the top, and walk straight on up Tower Street; at the first

View over the town from Launceston Castle

The ruins of **Launceston Castle** rise proudly above the town, and date from soon after the Norman Conquest. Most of what can be seen today dates from the 13th century when the castle was remodelled under instruction of Richard, Earl of Cornwall. The castle (which has never seen active service – though it changed hands five times during the Civil War, without resistance) also marks the western end of the Two Castles Trail, a long-distance walking route linking the Norman castles at Launceston and at Okehampton over the border in Devon.

bend to the left go straight ahead up wide railed steps to reach Castle Street.

D Turn right to pass the Lawrence House Museum (National Trust) on the right, a beautiful Georgian house dating from 1753 and built by Humphry Lawrence. The house was also the unofficial headquarters for French POWs during the Napoleonic wars, during which time Launceston was a parole town. Pass the Eagle House Hotel on the right, and follow the road as it veers left to pass an entrance to the castle. Follow the road on to pass the church of St Mary Magdalene on the left. Go down Church Street and into Southgate; one of the three entrance gates remaining from the time that Launceston was a walled town, Southgate was originally used as a prison. Walk up Race Hill; the car park is on the left.

St Agnes

START Carn Gowla
DISTANCE 3 miles (4.8km)
TIME 1½ hours
PARKING Car park (free) at Carn Gowla, just south of St Agnes Head
ROUTE FEATURES No difficulties

A glimpse into Cornwall's industrial past can be gained on this lovely route that leads along the magnificent cliffs around St Agnes Head to pass Wheal Coates, now in the hands of the National Trust, before ascending St Agnes Beacon. Keep this one for a clear day – the views all over north Cornwall from the top of the beacon are superb – and in late summer the cliffs and beacon glow purple under a carpet of heather.

🎵 From the car park walk through the line of granite boulders on a gritty track that runs along the cliffs at Tubby's Head, with fantastic views towards the sandy beaches at Chapel Porth and Porthtowan, and beyond to Godrevy Point.

Deep underground mining was carried out at **Wheal Coates** from the 1870s, concentrating on workings just below low-tide mark, and 138 people worked here in 1881. After various periods of closure and reopening, the mine finally ceased operation in 1914. The three largest buildings on the site are engine houses, and have been beautifully restored. The shaft from Towanroath is 600ft (183m) deep, and is (fortunately) protected by a grille today.

Ⓐ Where the coast path is signed right, keep straight ahead on a level track to reach the restored buildings at Wheal Coates. Note the gashes and gulleys in the heather and gorse en route, evidence of medieval opencast mining when tin-bearing veins (lodes) were dug out. Take some time to explore Wheal Coates;

PUBLIC TRANSPORT Bus services from Perranporth and Truro to St Agnes
REFRESHMENTS None on route; picnic area near St Agnes Head; wide range of pubs and cafés in St Agnes
PUBLIC TOILETS None on route
ORDNANCE SURVEY MAPS Explorer 104 (Redruth & St Agnes), Landranger 203 (Land's End & Isles of Scilly)

The views from the top of **St Agnes Beacon** stretch for more than 30 miles (48km) on a good day and legend has it that Giant Bolster could stand with one foot on the beacon, the other on Carn Brea. The trig point pillar dates from 1937 (there was a summerhouse here in the late 18th century), but the hill was identified as one of the Ordnance Survey's first trig stations in 1796. During the Napoleonic wars, a signal guard was stationed here to look out for invaders.

Stamps engine house

you will learn a huge amount about the history of Cornish tin-mining here.

> **?** *How high is St Agnes Beacon?*

B When you are ready to move on, continue in the same direction, passing between Stamps and Whim engine houses on a gritty path; look down the cliff at the impressive Towanroath engine house below right. The path drops down fairly steeply; ignore a small path coming in from the right; when your path reaches an obvious one running across in front of you turn left inland, slightly uphill. Follow the path to meet the gritty track to Wheal Coates car park, which is passed on the right, to meet the lane.

C Turn left; a little way up the lane, turn right up the drive for Beacon Cottage Farm touring park between granite gateposts. Keep on the drive to pass the farmhouse; veer right before entering the farmyard (camping field is on the right). Ahead there are three gateways: go through the one on the left and up the track into a grassy field. Where the hedgebank runs away left, go straight across the field, aiming for an open gateway in the next hedgebank. Walk up the next field, keeping the hedgebank left, and leave the field over a granite stile to gain the edge of the beacon. The area has long been a valuable source of very young sands and clays (under 50 million years); in times past clay was used to hold miners' candles when underground, securing them either on to rocks, or on to the miners' hats.

D Turn right on a well-trodden path, and stay on it as it veers left and climbs to the top of the beacon. Walk straight on from the beacon, taking the right of the two obvious paths along the ridge. Ignoring all small paths coming in from the right, keep going until the lane comes into view below right and an obvious path appears on the right, leading to the lane.

E Turn right along the lane and immediately left down a rough track; where it turns sharp right, go straight on to pass a metal

Looking towards Chapel Porth

barrier and over the bank ahead. Go straight across the first path to reach the coast path, with views to Bawden Rocks offshore, which has colonies of black-backed gulls, razorbills and guillemots. Turn left along the coast path back to Carn Gowla, passing the coastguard lookout at St Agnes Head on the way. ●

Map labels

St Agnes Head · 70 · Bawden Farm · Shaft (dis) · South West Coast Path · New Downs Farm · Shafts (dis) · New Downs · 51 · Higher Bal Farm · Mine (dis) · Quarry (dis) · High · Shaft (dis) · Cairn · St Agnes Beacon · Beacon Drive · Tubby's Head · Chy · Mine (dis) · Beacon Cottage Farm · Cave · Chy · Natural Arch · Cave · 50 · Chapel (rems of) · Goonvrea · 95 · PC · 72 · Parc-nor · Mine (dis) · Tips (dis) · P 4 Carn Gowla

5 St Catherine's Castle

The views over Fowey and Polruan, and up the Fowey River from St Catherine's Castle (a coastal fort), situated high above the sea on St Catherine's Head, have to be seen to be believed. This varied walk follows the coast path past secluded sandy coves to reach the 16th-century fort, which was built to protect the river-mouth from possible French attack.

START Coombe car park, west of Fowey
DISTANCE 2½ miles (4km)
TIME 1½ hours
PARKING National Trust car park at Coombe farm (50p honesty box)
ROUTE FEATURES Fairly strenuous coast path; several stiles

Leave the car park and turn left onto the lane, then left again down a green lane towards the sea (no footpath sign). Follow this broad, level track; it bends sharp right to end at a wooden gate into a field.

A Once through the gate turn left and walk around the edge of the field, following the hedge. There are good views ahead of the 84ft (25.6m) red-and-white striped daymark on Gribbin Head, built in 1832 as a navigational aid. Walk downhill to leave the field via a

St Catherine's Castle is managed by English Heritage, and is open all year round. It is a two-storey artillery fort, built in 1510, and later incorporated in Henry VIII's south coast defence system. This included larger castles at St Mawes and Pendennis Castle at Falmouth, both built to protect the Fal estuary, at that time the busiest port on the south coast. St Catherine's Castle was manned during the Civil War, refortified in the mid-19th century, and had anti-aircraft guns positioned there during World War II to protect craft massing in the estuary before the D-Day invasion.

PUBLIC TRANSPORT None available
REFRESHMENTS Sometimes available at Coombe Farm; café at Readymoney Cove (just off route); wide range of pubs and cafés in Fowey
PUBLIC TOILETS None on route; at Readymoney Cove
ORDNANCE SURVEY MAPS Explorer 107 (St Austell & Liskeard), Landranger 200 (Newquay & Bodmin)

small wooden gate onto a narrow track. This runs downhill under trees through another gate, and on to reach the coast path via a metal gate just east of secluded Polridmouth Cove, a great place for a spot of rockpooling. The pretty house is on the site of the old manorial corn mill for Menabilly, just inland, where the novelist Daphne Du Maurier lived for many years. Fowey celebrates her love of Cornwall by hosting the Daphne Du Maurier Festival of Arts & Literature every year in May. Note the stepping stones across the dam below the ornamental lake on the right.

B Turn left along the coast path to gain Lankelly Cliff up a flight of wooden steps and over a stile. Walk along the edge of the field, then climb up the next hill through an open gateway, with views of Polruan opening up ahead. The path drops down to a small cove and over a stile, then over the next field and down steep steps to reach Coombe Hawn. From there, it runs steeply uphill and over a stile to enter Allday's Fields. Pass through a small gate into Covington Wood; take the first narrow path to the

Typical Cornish hedgebank

Fowey from Polruan in holiday time

The church of **St Fimbarrus** in Fowey marks the end of the Saint's Way (Forth an Syns in Cornish), a 30-mile (48km) path that runs from the south door of Padstow parish church, on the north Cornish coast, and was conceived in 1984. It is thought to follow, in part at least, the line of an ancient cross-county route that linked a number of important religious sites.

right, and follow it onto St Catherine's Point; look carefully at the opposite headland to see the ruins of St Saviour's Chapel. Take the path veering left, then right to the castle entrance. There are wonderful views over Readymoney Cove, Fowey and upriver from here. Fowey took over from Lostwithiel as the main seaport for the area in the late 14th century, but in turn was superseded by Truro by the 15th. It is still a major port for the export of china clay, and the river buzzes with all kinds of maritime activity.

C Retrace your steps into Allday's Fields, and turn right uphill across the field, passing a wooden seat on the left. The path runs on through an open gateway and wooden stile onto a track to pass Coombe Farm on the left; continue up the lane to reach the car park on the left.

? *When were Allday's Fields given to the people of Fowey, and by whom?*

St Ives

START St Ives
DISTANCE 2¼ miles (3.6km)
TIME 1¼ hours (plus
1 hour)
PARKING Barnoon upper
car park (fee-paying),
signposted for Tate St Ives
and Porthmeor beach
ROUTE FEATURES No
difficulties

6

The popular seaside town of St Ives has drawn both artists and holiday-makers for many years, attracted by the fantastic quality of light, beautiful coastline and wonderful sandy beaches. You can experience a little of everything St Ives has to offer on this walk, which leads past the Tate St Ives gallery out to lovely Clodgy Point, and back to the bustling town via quiet tracks and lanes.

Leave the car park by the public toilets and take the steps which lead steeply down to Beach Road, running along the back of Porthmeor beach. The Tate St Ives, built on the site of an old gas-works, can be found just to the right: this spectacular building, opened in June 1993, was designed and built by Eldred Evans and David Shalev. The gallery houses exhibitions of works produced by St Ives artists from the late 1880s to the present day.

One of the prime figures of the 'plein air' movement which drew artists to **St Ives** was Ben Nicholson (1894–1982), one of Britain's major abstract artists, who came here on holiday with fellow-artist Christopher Wood (1901–30) in 1928. Nicholson moved here in 1939 with his wife, the sculptor Barbara Hepworth (1903–75). Over the next two decades they turned St Ives into one of the leading centres of British art.

A Turn left; when the toilets are reached on the right, leave the pavement and take the broad

PUBLIC TRANSPORT Bus service from Camborne, Helston, Lands End, Newquay, Penzance, Redruth and Truro
REFRESHMENTS Wide range of pubs and cafés in St Ives; café and restaurant at the Tate St Ives
PUBLIC TOILETS Barnoon car park and by Porthmeor beach
ORDNANCE SURVEY MAPS Explorer 102 (Land's End), Landranger 203 (Land's End & Isles of Scilly)

the lighthouse on Godrevy Island. Pass through a kissing gate and walk out to the end of Clodgy Point ('clodgy' means 'leper' in Cornish). Turn inland, uphill across Burthallan Cliff; rejoin the path and turn right uphill, aiming for a wooden seat. Keep going uphill to reach a coast path post, signed right.

> **?** *Across the road from the start of the tarmac walkway on point A you pass an old well. To whom is it dedicated?*

Glorious summer colour

tarmac walkway that runs below the road to pass Porthmeor Bowling Club, and on across a grassy area. Follow the coast path signs along the now gritty path; look back for fantastic views over The Island and across St Ives Bay to

B Leave the coast path and walk straight on uphill. The narrow, tussocky path leads through bracken and gorse; where it forks, keep straight on to reach Higher Burthallan House on the right. Pass through a metal five-bar gate and onto an earthy track; look out for superb views over St Ives Bay to the

The Tate St Ives from Carrick Du

Nicholson and Wood 'discovered' local mariner and artist **Alfred Wallis** (1855–1942), who took up painting at the age of 70 to occupy him after his wife's death. His primitive paintings are some of the best-known from the St Ives School, yet this modest man never regarded himself as a 'proper artist'. His cottage can be found on the left of Back Road West, a little way past the Tate St Ives, towards The Island.

left. The track becomes tarmac at Fairview Farmhouse; walk along the lane to pass the Garrack Hotel and meet the road.

C Turn left downhill, and follow the road towards the centre of St Ives. This picturesque old fishing town's original claim to fame was that it was Cornwall's most important pilchard-fishing port, until the demise of the industry in the early 20th century. It is well worth exploring the narrow lanes, courtyards and alleyways between Porthmeor beach and the harbour, where (out of season) you can get a real feeling of what life must have been like here in the 18th and 19th centuries, before the holiday trade took over. Where the road bends sharp right and downhill, cross over (with Barnoon cemetery on the left) and go straight on to find the car park on the left.

7 *Tintagel*

START St Materiana's Church

DISTANCE 2 miles (3.2km)

TIME 1 hour

PARKING Car park (free) by St Materiana's Church, signposted from the centre of Tintagel village

ROUTE FEATURES Coast path undulating; steep descent to castle entrance; field paths sometimes muddy

It's not hard to get carried away with romantic notions as you gaze over the ruins of Tintagel Castle, magnificently situated on the north Cornish coast, where tales of King Arthur abound. Our route leads along the coast path to the castle entrance, then runs around craggy Barras Nose, with glorious views all around, before returning via Tintagel village.

From the car park walk north-east along the well-marked coast path, passing St Materiana's Church on the right. Almost immediately, views of the flat-topped island on which part of the castle is built, rising 250ft (76m) above the sea, open up ahead and left. The path drops down a flight of uneven steps and through a break in the hedgebank to leave Glebe Cliff by an NT contributions cairn.

A Walk downhill to reach the upper entrance to the castle (under

St Materiana has been identified with St Madryn, a Welsh princess said to have been active in this part of Cornwall around AD 500. The 12th-century church, set in splendid isolation on Glebe Cliff, is thought to have been built on the site of an oratory which was linked to her main shrine at Minster, a few miles inland. The discovery of 5th-century slate-lined graves at the church indicate that this could have been a burial site for important people, presumably from the castle.

the care of English Heritage), then follow coast path signs right and sharp left to zigzag down to reach

PUBLIC TRANSPORT Bus service from Bodmin, Bude, Exeter, Launceston, Okehampton, Tavistock, Truro, Wadebridge

REFRESHMENTS Castle Beach café (April to October) at castle entrance, wide range of pubs and cafés in Tintagel

PUBLIC TOILETS At castle entrance; in Tintagel village

ORDNANCE SURVEY MAPS Explorer 111 (Bude, Boscastle & Tintagel), Landranger 200 (Newquay & Bodmin)

St Materiana's church

and it is likely that Tintagel was occupied by someone of great importance until the 8th century, when it was abandoned.

> For generations **Tintagel** has been linked with legends of King Arthur and the Knights of the Round Table. It is easy to understand why when you visit the castle and let your imagination wander: it's a wonderfully evocative place. Although several sites share the claim, many believe that Arthur was born here. He is most likely to have been a powerful warrior famed for his battles against Saxon invaders.

the main track to the castle, with the public toilets on the left. Turn left to pass the English Heritage shop on the left, and the café across the stream on the right, to reach the sea at Tintagel Haven, from where you can gaze in awe at the ruined walls and buildings on the island towering above you. Most of the visible ruins date from the 13th century, when Richard, Earl of Cornwall, carried out a massive refortification of this naturally defensive site. There is evidence of Celtic occupation here too,

B Turn right to cross the stream on a footbridge, then up steep steps, following coast path signs slightly uphill.

Pass a National Trust sign indicating that you have reached Barras Nose, then follow the path downhill over a footbridge. Take the path leading left to reach the end of the Barras Nose headland, with wonderful views of the castle to the left, and towards the next headland, Willapark, to the right.

Looking over Tintagel Haven from Barras Nose

> **?** *When was Barras Nose purchased by the National Trust, and why?*

C Retrace your steps inland to rejoin the coast path and keep left to pass through a wooden gate. The narrow path runs along Smith's Cliff through heather and bracken, then veers inland as a grassy area is reached, to pass two footpath posts. At the second post the coast path is signed left; turn right slightly uphill, keeping the hedgebank on the left. At the top of the rise go over a wooden stile and straight along the field; over the next stile, and across a stream on stone slabs (wet in winter). Leave that field over a stone slab stile onto a hedged farm track, which meets a tarmac lane by Headland camping and caravanning park on the left.

D Walk straight on along the lane through busy Tintagel village, which is best negotiated quickly and can be a shock after the majesty of the castle and coastline. The lane curves sharp left to pass the track to the castle (right); turn right down the next lane, signposted St Materiana's Church. At the bottom of the hill, look out for the tiny 13th/14th-century Chapel of Our Lady of Fontevrault (open weekdays), built into the vicarage gatehouse. Continue up the lane, and back to your car. ●

Trelissick

START Trelissick Garden

DISTANCE 2¾ miles (4.4km)

TIME 1¾ hours

PARKING National Trust car park at Trelissick Garden (£1.50, NT members free)

ROUTE FEATURES Fairly steep climb from Lamouth Creek to road opposite Trelissick; some paths muddy after wet weather; dogs to be kept on a lead near the house

8

Starting from the National Trust's beautiful gardens at Trelissick, this gentle walk runs through mature parkland, then along the wooded Fal estuary to the King Harry Ferry. Turning inland to follow a peaceful woodland path overlooking picturesque Lamouth Creek, the route climbs up to re-enter the Trelissick estate at the Old Lodge.

Walk out of the car park, just past the information board on the left, turn left on a broad, tarmac path to pass through a small gate by the cattle grid to enter the park, with lovely views down the Fal estuary – also known as the Carrick Roads (from 'caryk rood', rocky harbour) – the third-largest natural harbour in the world.

A Cross the drive that leads to the house, and walk downhill across open grassy parkland towards the left side of Channals Creek. The

Trelissick House was built around 1750 and sold in 1805 to mining entrepreneur Ralph Daniel. In the early 19th century his son Thomas laid out the extensive carriage drives that run through the estate. The Gilbert family took over in 1844 and further developed the house, but the beautiful gardens were largely created by Leonard Cunliffe, his stepdaughter Ida Copeland, and her husband Ronald. The gardens are famous for their tender exotic plants, encouraged by their sheltered position and mild climate. The 376-acre (152ha) estate was given to the National Trust in 1955.

PUBLIC TRANSPORT Bus service from Truro

REFRESHMENTS National Trust café at Trelissick (February to Christmas); the Punchbowl & Ladle pub at Penelewey (north-west of Trelissick)

PUBLIC TOILETS Opposite the National Trust shop at Trelissick (February to Christmas)

ORDNANCE SURVEY MAPS Explorer 105 (Falmouth & Mevagissey), Landranger 204 (Truro & Falmouth)

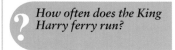

park was laid out in the mid-18th century to complement the first house, built by John Lawrence, which has since been extended, and is not open to the public.

B At the sea wall at Channals Creek (where there is access to the beach) turn left to pass through an iron kissing gate and follow the narrow, gritty path under twisted oak and sweet chestnut trees along the edge of the River Fal. This lovely, level path leads through South Wood, and has the added interest of all kinds of vessels passing by on the water. As the woodland below Trelissick Garden is reached the woodland becomes dark, damp and leafy, with holly and laurel, and the path drops steps to reach the King Harry Ferry, which began operating in 1889 and links the west side of the Fal with the Roseland Peninsula. The original ferry operated from 1889 until 1913; the present ferry was built at Penryn in 1974.

> **?** *How often does the King Harry ferry run?*

C Walk a little way left up the lane, then turn right up steps into North Wood. The path levels off to

The remains of an Iron Age fort have been found above **Roundwood Quay** (which can be seen across Lamouth Creek), the earliest evidence of prehistoric settlement here, and probably built to control the upper reaches of the Fal. The 18th century wharves at the quay were used for shipping out tin and copper, which was smelted and refined on site, and in the mid-19th century the quay was still the scene of some activity, with a malt house, lime kiln and shipbuilding.

run along the edge of pretty Lamouth Creek, where this joins the Fal it forms Britain's largest deep-water harbour, as evidenced by the number of huge ocean-going vessels that lie up here, and which add an unexpected element to this route. Follow the path to a junction, with Roundwood fort and quay signed ahead and right; turn left, away from the creek, signed Trelissick. The path zigzags very steeply uphill to reach the road at a wooden gate.

D Cross the road with care, to re-enter the Trelissick parkland by the early 19th-century neo-Grecian Old Lodge, and walk straight on through Old Lodge beech plantation. The path veers left and downhill to meet the drive to the house. Turn left through a wooden gate by the cattle grid and follow the drive through open parkland, which has a wonderfully informal and relaxing feel. The drive veers left and back to starting point of the walk at the car park.   ●

View across Channals Creek

9 *Coverack*

START Coverack
DISTANCE 4½ miles (7.2km)
TIME 2½ hours
PARKING Car park (fee-paying) in Coverack; also St Keverne parish council charity car park (20p honesty box)
ROUTE FEATURES Coast path occasionally boggy; twisty through quarries

A walk along the coast path as it runs north-east from the picturesque old fishing village of Coverack is quite a surprise, as the coast here is low-lying and somewhat 'un-Cornish' in character. The walk passes a working quarry, then runs inland along quiet lanes to reach the delights of Roskilly's ice-cream at Tregellast Barton – definitely worth the effort of getting there.

Walk downhill from the car park towards the sea.

A Turn left along the tarmac lane signed coast path. The lane becomes a gritty track and ends at a five-bar gate; turn right down the narrow, coast path through trees, and over a stile onto the open low-lying cliff. The coast runs over various banks, stiles and stepping-stones to reach flat Lowland Point, a raised beach dating from an interglacial period within the last Ice Age when the sea level was higher. The steep hill inland was the original cliff. Lowland Point also has evidence of prehistoric occupation in the form of field boundaries and hut remains.

The old fishing village of **Coverack** had a thriving pilchard fishing fleet from medieval times to the early years of the 20th century, and also a fairly healthy reputation for smuggling. A lifeboat was stationed here until 1963, largely on account of **The Manacles** (see panel opposite).

The rather grand-sounding Paris Hotel is named after the *Paris*, which was stranded off the coast in 1899.

PUBLIC TRANSPORT Bus service from Truro
REFRESHMENTS Paris Hotel, Harbour Lights café and Fodder Barn tearooms in Coverack; Croust House restaurant and café at Roskilly's
PUBLIC TOILETS In the car park; also at Roskilly's
ORDNANCE SURVEY MAPS Explorer 103 (The Lizard), Landranger 203 (Land's End & Isles of Scilly)

B Follow the coast path on to Dean quarries, where gabbro – an igneous rock used widely as roadstone and in coastal defence building – is mined. A notice gives details of blasting and warning signals. Make sure you follow the marked path carefully through the quarry, as it does occasionally alter, and leads eventually to a lorry turning area. Follow the footpath signs past

The craggy rocks visible off Lowland Point are the infamous **Manacles**, particularly dangerous to shipping as they are almost submerged at high tide. Before radar was invented, ships tended to hug the coast, and The Manacles have claimed many victims over the centuries, including the *John*, wrecked in 1855 en route from Plymouth to Canada, with the loss of 196 lives. In 1898 the *Mohegan* foundered on the rocks, and more than 100 passengers and crew lie buried in St Keverne churchyard. Interestingly. St Keverne's church tower is a mix of tower and spire, with the intention of creating a very obvious landmark to warn mariners away from The Manacles.

The picturesque harbour at Coverack

storage bays to join the gritty access road; where that bends sharp left go straight on downhill towards Godrevy Cove, from where the notorious Long Meadow Gang of smugglers operated in the 18th century. The indistinct path runs along the back of the beach.

> **?** *When does blasting take place at Dean quarries, and how would you know it was going to happen?*

C When almost at the far end, turn left and walk inland, aiming for the right end of a patch of bullrushes growing against the low cliffs. The path crosses a stream on a wooden footbridge; go up the steps, through the metal gate, and up the field, keeping the hedge and stream on the right. At the next open gateway the path veers away left between high hedgebanks; cross the Cornish stile at the top of the field, and walk up large granite steps right and through an old metal gate to enter sycamore woodland. The path ends with Chynhale on the left. Turn right, and walk along the lane into the hamlet of Rosenithon.

D At the T-junction turn left (coast path signed right). Just before the end of the lane, turn left over a stile into a Countryside Stewardship area. Keep left at the first fork and walk on past ornamental lakes to reach a gate at a crossroads. Go straight over to find the Tudor farmstead at Tregellast Barton, a working farm and now home to Roskilly's, a successful farm produce business, best known for its delicious ice-cream.

E Continue past Roskilly's; at the entrance to Trebarveth farm (left), turn left over a Cornish stile, signed Coverack. Walk diagonally across the field, over a Cornish stile and along the edge of the next field, inside a wire fence. Go over another Cornish stile at the end and straight on, keeping the hedge on the left. Over the next hedgebank, and straight on across the field, aiming for another hedgebank coming in from the left. Follow that hedgebank to leave the

field over a Cornish stile; cross the next field diagonally, aiming for the top left corner. Leave over a Cornish stile; turn right onto the lane at Trevalsoe.

F Where the lane bends right, turn left following a footpath post/arrow. Walk through a strip of woodland and over a stone stile to reach Boscarnon. Follow the track to the left of the house and walk down the drive, which becomes a concrete lane. Where the lane bends right, turn left over the stile in the hedgebank. Once in the field, walk left through a gap in the hedge and straight ahead through another gap. Walk straight on, aiming for a gap in the top right corner, to pass under big sycamore trees. Follow footpath posts through an open grassy area, then into woodland, and over a Cornish stile and hedgebank to join the coast path. Turn right and retrace your steps back to the car park in Coverack. ●

Inside the harbour wall

10 *Geevor and Levant*

START Pendeen lighthouse
DISTANCE 3½ miles (5.6km)
TIME 1¾ hours
PARKING Pendeen lighthouse, signposted from the B3306 in Pendeen
ROUTE FEATURES Indistinct, slightly overgrown path from Geevor to Boscaswell

Every visitor to Cornwall should take some time to learn about the county's past, and in this remote and sometimes desolate part of West Penwith there is plenty of evidence of her industrial heritage, stamped on a stunning natural coastline – it's an area that really makes you think. The walk leads through the fascinating remains of the Geevor and Levant tin mines, now partly restored and open to the public.

The **Levant** mine closed in 1930, and its workings are now flooded by the sea. Take some time to have a look at Levant's indoor beam engine, the oldest surviving example in Cornwall. It was built by Harvey's of Hayle and has been restored by the Trevithick Society. Owned by the National Trust, there are regular steaming days throughout the year. The Levant mining disaster exhibition also offers a dramatic insight into the hardships and dangers of this 2,000-year-old industry.

From Pendeen lighthouse walk along the lane inland to reach the coastguard cottages on the left. The lighthouse was built in 1900 to augment the Longships and Trevose lighthouses, views of which could be obscured by high cliffs from certain angles. The lighthouse, run by the Trevithick Trust, is sometimes open to the public. It holds the largest surviving siren fog signal in Britain. It was automated in 1995.

🅐 Opposite cottage No 6 turn right by the granite marker signed Cape Cornwall; follow the coast path downhill to cross a stream on

PUBLIC TRANSPORT Bus service from Penzance and St Just (to Pendeen)
REFRESHMENTS None on route; shop/post office in Higher Boscaswell
PUBLIC TOILETS None on main route; opposite shop in Higher Boscaswell
ORDNANCE SURVEY MAPS Explorer 102 (Land's End), Landranger 203 (Land's End & Isles of Scilly)

stone steps. Walk uphill and over two stiles to reach Carn Ros; look ahead for good views of the Victorian settling tanks, chimneys and buildings connected with the old tin mines at Trewellard Bottoms. The greenish stain on the cliffs ahead indicates the presence of copper. Follow the coast path signs around the back of the cove, then uphill to pass a sign to Geevor to the left, with Levant signed straight on. Follow the coast path to reach the entrance to Levant beam engine on the right.

B Turn left by the car park for Levant and walk inland up quiet Levant Road to reach the edge of Trewellard. Just past the 30mph sign, turn left by Pentrew. Follow the lane straight on to pass Merrivale House on the left. Keep straight on to pass through farm buildings; the lane becomes a

The **Geevor Heritage Centre** is a good example of how an uneconomic enterprise can be turned into a popular tourist attraction. Geevor was the last surviving mine in the area, and is the largest preserved mine site in the UK. Known as East Levant in the 19th century, it closed in 1840 and reopened in 1951 until final closure in 1990. It was renamed Wheal Geevor (a name first recorded in the early 18th century) at the end of the 19th century, and at its height employed more than 400 men.

Geevor and Levant WALK 10

Crowns engine house, Botallack

inaccessible stone stile on the path, veer left to avoid it and continue up the field, keeping the hedge on the right. The Geevor Heritage Centre buildings can be clearly seen to the right; most of these are 20th century, and now house the museum, café and shop. You can also visit the late 19th-century carpenter's shop and stables, and the 1850s count house (the original mine offices). Walk through a gap in the wall at the top of the field onto a broad grassy track between low stone walls.

track, then reduces to a narrow path between low walls. Follow this downhill; look right towards the restored mine buildings at Geevor. This path ends at a T-junction with a huge boulder to the left; climb over the bank straight ahead, and walk downhill (with a wire fence on the right) to rejoin the coast path at Trewellard Bottoms by the Geevor/Levant signpost passed earlier.

D When the houses at the edge of Lower Boscaswell are reached, go straight ahead on the track, which becomes a tarmac lane; walk on to pass a small parking area on the right. This quiet country lane leaves the hamlet and eventually joins the road to Pendeen light-house opposite Calartha Farm. Turn left and follow the road back past the coastguard cottages to your car. ●

C Turn right and walk along the coast path; where it soon turns sharp left towards the sea at the back of the cove, leave the coast path and walk straight ahead and slightly uphill to follow a footpath post with a green arrow. The path is narrow and a little overgrown, with a post-and-wire fence to the right. When you reach an

? *What is the name of the house at Pendeen Gate?*

The Lizard to Church Cove

START The Lizard

DISTANCE 3½ miles (5.6km)

TIME 1¾ hours

PARKING National Trust car park near Lizard Point (£1.30, NT members free)

ROUTE FEATURES Uneven steps down to Housel Bay; steep climb up lane from Church Cove to Landewednack

This refreshing walk, starting from mainland England's southernmost point, meanders along the cliff top, glorious with wildflowers in summer, past some fascinating features – the Lizard lighthouse, the chasm of the Lion's Den, Lloyd's signal station and the lifeboat station at Kilcobben Cove – before turning inland to return via the lovely church of St Wynwallow.

The signal station at **Bass Point** was built in 1872 by shipping agents G.C. Fox & Co, and is further evidence of the strategic significance of the Lizard peninsula. More than 1,000 ships a month were using the station by 1878. Part of the building was leased to Lloyd's of London in 1883, to report the arrival of ships from across the Atlantic to London. Since 1992 it has been in the hands of the National Trust.

? *What was the name of the first lifeboat to carry out a rescue in this area, and when?*

From the car park walk towards the sea on a gritty path, past the NT information boards. Pass the toilets on the left, and walk down steps; at the next junction of paths turn right, then down railed steps to reach the coast path.

A Turn right and go to have a look at Lizard Point which, despite its famed position at 49° 57' N latitude, and 5° 12' W longitude, is something of a disappointment. But the coastal scenery is fantastic,

PUBLIC TRANSPORT Bus service from Truro via Helston

REFRESHMENTS Polpeor Café and Wave Crest Café at Lizard Point; cafés, fish and chips and Top House pub in Lizard village

PUBLIC TOILETS In car park and signposted off green in Lizard village

CHILDREN'S PLAY AREA Opposite Beacon Terrace, towards the end of the walk

ORDNANCE SURVEY MAPS Explorer 103 (The Lizard), Landranger 203 (Land's End & Isles of Scilly)

Map labels:

Parn Voose Cove
Chapel Lane (Track)
A3083
13
Cross Common
Quarry (dis)
The Balk
Church Cove
Carn Caerthillian
NT
76
Church Cove
Kilcobben Cove
C NT
Sch
Cross
D
Lizard
PO
63
Tregaminion
62
Lifeboat Station
Prilla Cove
Green Lane
Hot Point
Lloyds Road
62
Housel Bay
71
69
Pyg
Hotel
Coastguard Station
Park-an-Castle
NT
12
NT
SWC Path
Housel Cove
NT
Bass Point
P **11**
NT
Lizard Point
70
Lizard Lighthouse
PC
NT
Laven-a-caen
Bolijack
Housel Bay
Lion's Den
Pen Olver
Barges Rock
Shag Rock
B 34 **A**
Bumble Rock
Polpeor Cove
Polbream Cove
Man of War
Vellan Drang
Mên Par
Labham Rock
Pen Ervan
1 KM
HALF MILE
0

and in the summer the cliffs glow yellow and magenta under a blanket of mysenbryanthemum (Hottentot fig). There are also a couple of interesting serpentine workshops here: some believe that the name 'Lizard' derives in part from the underlying rock of the peninsula which, when wet, resembles the skin of a snake. Look out, too, for the old lifeboat station in Polpeor Cove to the west, which ran from 1859 to 1961.

B From Lizard Point retrace your steps along the coast path to pass the steps back to the car park. The path runs below the lighthouse, built in 1752 to oversee one of the busiest shipping lanes in the world;

it became automated in 1999. The path runs along the cliff to pass the Lion's Den to the right, formed in 1842 when the roof of a sea cave collapsed, and on to drop steeply down steps to the back of Housel Cove. Cross the stream on a concrete bridge, and follow the path up steps; at the next junction

St Wynwallow

of paths turn right on the coast path to pass below the gardens of the Housel Bay hotel. Walk on towards Pen Olver, passing to the right of the experimental Marconi wireless station, set up in 1900, and then on the broad grassy path to pass the voluntary National Coastwatch station and Lloyd's signal station at Bass Point. Keep on the coast path to pass a pink house on the left; a little down the track, turn right and follow the coast path along the cliffs to Kilcobben Cove. Walk up the steps to reach the Lizard lifeboat station.

RNLI lifeboats were stationed at **Polpeor Cove** until 1961, and at **Cadgwith** from 1867–1963; there was also one for a brief time at Church Cove at the end of the 19th century. The new station at Kilcobben Cove was built in 1958 in a sheltered position from which launching can take place in any weather conditions. A board near the station lists all those rescues carried out in the area since the mid-19th century – it is an incredible record.

C Follow the coast path past the lifeboat station to reach pretty Church Cove – formerly the site of a pilchard fishery – at a concrete walkway. Turn right to have a look at the cove, then walk straight up the walkway which runs steeply uphill past thatched cottages. The ancient church of St Wynwallow, with its squat serpentine tower, is passed on the right; there is thought to have been a church here since about AD 600, and parts of the existing building date to the 12th century, followed by refurbishments in the 13th, 15th and 19th centuries. Situated in the parish of Landewednack, it is the most southerly place of worship in England. It was here that the last sermon in Cornish was delivered, in 1670. Follow the lane on; at the fork by The Forge, keep left on the main lane to reach a T-junction.

D Turn left to pass Cross Common nursery on the right (with its impressive range of exotic plants). Opposite the school and Beacon Terrace (right), turn left over the hedgebank on stone steps, signed public footpath. Walk diagonally across the field, aiming for the corner of the playing field on the right, then turn right, keeping the hedgebank on the right. The path veers round the end of the field and through a kissing gate. Pass the farmyard on the left, down a gritty track and round a metal gate to meet the road. Cross the road and follow the footpath, which runs parallel to the road and then crosses it to lead back to the car park. ●

12 *Morwenstow*

START Church of St Morwenna & St John the Baptist, Morwenstow

DISTANCE 4 miles (6.4km)

TIME 2½ hours

PARKING National Trust car park by the church (contributions cairn)

ROUTE FEATURES Very steep and strenuous coast path from Stanbury Mouth to Vicarage Cliff, and precipitous cliffs; take care

The remote hamlet of Morwenstow, lying just 2 miles (3.2km) from the Devon border, is a gem, and well worth investigating. Don't be misled by the easy start to this walk, which runs across wooded combes and farmland to Stanbury Mouth: the return along the coast path is hard work, but the views and sense of space repay every ounce of effort.

From the car park walk back up the lane away from the church, to reach the green at Crosstown.

Ⓐ Turn right and walk through the gate to the right of the Bush Inn, originally a monks' resthouse and dating in part from AD 950. Cross the stile, bottom left, and, almost immediately, over another to the right to enter the Tidna valley. Walk left downhill to a stile leading into sycamore woodland, and down wooden steps. Ignore the path straight ahead; turn left over a stile and stream. Follow the

Hawker's lovely church of **St Morwenna & St John the Baptist** (there are two holy wells dedicated to these saints nearby) is the most northerly parish church in Cornwall. It was enlarged in the 16th and 17th centuries, and its pinnacled tower provided a useful landmark from the sea in times past. There are three beautiful Norman arches in the nave, with typical zigzag moulding. The Victorian Gothic style rectory, seen just below the church, was built by Hawker; its chimneys are modelled on the various church towers he had come across during his life.

path up the other side of the combe and over a stile, then over another

---

PUBLIC TRANSPORT Bus service from Bude and Holsworthy

REFRESHMENTS Bush Inn at Morwenstow; Rectory Tearooms (seasonal) by the church

PUBLIC TOILETS Behind the church; at the Bush Inn and Rectory Tearooms

ORDNANCE SURVEY MAPS Explorer 126 (Clovelly & Hartland), Landranger 190 (Bude & Clovelly)

into a field. Walk straight on, keeping the hedge left, and over the next stile. Cross the field to enter a narrow strip of woodland over a stile, then over two more to hit the track to the right of ornamental gates leading to the medieval manor house at Tonacombe.

B Cross the track and over a stile; walk up the field, over a stile into the next, and straight over the next, with views of the intrusive Composite Signals Organisation Station at Cleave Camp on the cliffs ahead, and over two stiles onto the lane at Stanbury farm. Turn left, and almost immediately right (unmarked) down the drive; at the edge of the yard in front of the house turn left down a fenced track, with a pond on the right, to a field gate. Walk uphill, veering right, and over a Cornish stile; at the end of the next field, cross the stile just by the lane and entrance to Eastway Manor (left).

C Turn right, keeping the hedgebank on the right. Leave the field over a double stile, downhill across the next field, and over a stile into a wooded combe. Walk over the footbridge and stile; at the crossroads of paths turn left down a rough path. Pass through a wooden gate and over a stile into the next field and straight on, then over a stile to meet a green lane on a bend. Turn left; the lane (sometimes boggy) ends at a stile; follow the narrow path downhill to meet the coast path. Go straight

The Caledonia's figurehead

on, cross the footbridge and pick your way carefully down to the rocky beach at Stanbury Mouth. The coast from Bude to Hartland Point is a geologist's dream, a complex, fascinating, almost lunar, succession of vertical tiltings and contortions dating back some 300 million years, broken up by a number of deeply-incised valleys.

D Return to the coast path. Turn left steeply uphill, and through a gate at the top. Take care along this stretch: the cliffs are unstable. Go over several stiles, then two footbridges and a stile. The next stile leads onto Higher Sharpnose Point; follow the path straight on to pass the old coastguard lookout, from where there are views to Hartland Quay to the north, once a vital lifeline for this remote part of Devon, but destroyed by the

ravages of the sea in the late 19th century. The coast path drops steeply down over a stile, and then to the stream at Tidna Shute. The last sighting of the large blue butterfly, extinct in 1979, was in the Tidna valley.

E Follow the coast path very steeply up onto Vicarage Cliff, and through a kissing gate. Almost immediately, turn left to find Hawker's Hut, with wonderful views over Lucky Hole. Continue along the coast path, through a kissing gate, and turn right inland. Go through two kissing gates; where the hedgebank veers right, cross the field towards the church, and over a Cornish stile into the churchyard. Take the path rising right from the south door, out through the lych gate, and back to the car. Look out for the ghostly white figurehead of the *Caledonia* to the right of the path, wrecked in 1842, which marks the graves of her captain and crew. ●

> **?** Whose kissing gate can be found on the edge of Vicarage Cliff, and who is responsible for placing it there?

Mount Edgcumbe

START Maker church
DISTANCE 4 miles (6.4km)
TIME 2 hours
PARKING Country park upper car park, near Maker Church
ROUTE FEATURES Steep through woods towards Millbrook creek; steeply undulating path (with many steps); dogs to be kept under close control in places.

This is a walk of real contrasts: a fascinating exploration of a peaceful and little-known corner of Cornwall, far off the beaten track yet lying just across the water from the bustling city of Plymouth, in Devon, and easily accessible by ferry. The route goes through the lovely Mount Edgcumbe country park and gardens, with wonderful views across Plymouth Sound.

Leave the car park out of the entrance, passing Maker Church on the left, to reach a footpath post (signed Empacombe and Cremyll ferry).

> **What is the name of the Cremyll ferry?**

A Turn right downhill to reach a wooden gate onto a lane; go down steps into sycamore woodland. Follow footpath posts which zigzag steeply downhill to cross a track, passing a disused quarry, left. At the bottom of the woods, turn left through a kissing gate into a field. Walk straight on, with lovely views ahead to Torpoint, with Brunel's iron railway bridge over the Tamar at Saltash. Join a track at the bottom of the field; go through a kissing gate on to the lane.

B Cross the lane and over the stile, with Millbrook Lake to the left. The level path runs along the field edge to pass through a kissing gate, with a ruined windmill to the

PUBLIC TRANSPORT Bus service from Plymouth (to Cremyll only)
REFRESHMENTS Edgcumbe Inn at Cremyll, refreshments at Cremyll ferry and entrance to country park, Orangery Restaurant in Mount Edgcumbe gardens (open daily during season 10.30am–4pm)
PUBLIC TOILETS At Cremyll, and near the Orangery Restaurant
ORDNANCE SURVEY MAPS Explorer 108 (Lower Tamar Valley & Plymouth), Landranger 201 (Plymouth & Launceston)

right. Walk along the bottom of the next field, and over a stile to tranquil private Empacombe Quay, where the components for the second Eddystone lighthouse were put together in the early 17th century. Be sure to keep to the waymarked route around the back of the harbour, then to the left of Harbourside House through an open gateway (the drive to Empacombe House), with great views over Devonport. Walk through an open gateway at the bottom of the next field; ignore the path leading right; keep left through a kissing gate to pass a derelict Admiralty pumping station. The path leads through another kissing gate into an open

The gardens and country park at **Mount Edgcumbe** are open all year round, and cover 860 acres (350ha). The formal gardens near Cremyll were laid out in the 18th century, as were the Earl's Garden near the house, and the Earl's Drive, which runs west from the house through the park to Penlee Point. The gardens are peppered with follies and grottos. The fallow deer that can sometimes be seen in the park are descendants of the herd originally established in the 16th century.

The Cremyll ferry, with Stonehouse beyond

field, and back into woodland over a wide metal stile, with an 18th-century obelisk (navigation aid) to the right. When the path meets a gritty track; turn left to pass a car park (right). The track meets the road at Cremyll, opposite the foot ferry, with the monumental 19th-century Stonehouse Barracks over the water. The Edgcumbe Arms is to the left.

C Turn right on the road (the coast path, though unsigned). Where the road veers right, walk straight ahead through the gates of Mount Edgcumbe country park (the small side gate is always open). Turn left; look right to see the house at the top end of a lovely horse-chestnut avenue. Pass through the gatehouse and the

Orangery Restaurant; follow the path straight on to reach the seawall and a blockhouse (1540) near the battery at Wilderness Point. Walk on past a huge ilex hedge (right), planted around 1700 to protect the gardens from salt spray. Pass through a gate to leave the formal gardens, and along the back of Barn Pool (used for tank embarkation during the World War II invasion of France). Look across to Plymouth Hoe and Drake's Island (originally known as St Nicholas' Island, after its chapel), which once housed a prison, then re-enter woodland by Milton's Temple. Pass through a wooden gate and follow footpath posts to reach a steep zigzag route with long flights of steps uphill, over a stile to pass a folly, then steeply

Mount Edgcumbe House was built from 1547–53 by Richard Edgcumbe of Cotehele, and was occupied by the Edgcumbe family until 1987. It was gutted by incendiary bombs on 22 April 1941, but the outer walls survived. The house was restored by Adrian Gilbert Scott between 1958–64, when the remaining red Tudor walls, granite window frames, 17th-century entrance door and 18th-century corner towers were incorporated into the fabric of the new building.

downhill to reach a woodland track. Follow this around the back of Picklecombe Point with its fort and quay. The track splits; keep left downhill through a five-bar gate to meet the lane. The old smuggling villages of Kingsand and Cawsand can be seen ahead, lying either side of the pre-1844 Devon/Cornwall border; the place names on the Rame peninsula tend to be Old English rather than Cornish.

D Turn right along the lane and follow it steeply inland up the Hoolake valley. Just before Maker farm, turn right through a gate, signed Maker Church. Cross the field (right of the telegraph pole), and through a kissing gate; cross the next field, aiming for the stile to the left of the white house. Go straight on (garden to the right), through a wooden gate; cross a stile and turn immediately right, keeping the hedgebank on the left. Climb over a railed Cornish stile and turn right towards the church; rejoin the lane to the car park. ●

By the Orangery Restaurant

Porthcurno and Treen

START Porthcurno
DISTANCE 3½ miles (5.6km)
TIME 1¾ hours
PARKING Car park (fee-paying) at Porthcurno beach
ROUTE FEATURES Steep walk up lane to the Minack Theatre; coast path narrow and rocky above Treen Cove

14

The white sands and turquoise sea at Porthcurno draw hundreds of holiday-makers on a sunny day. But it is easy to escape the crowds and explore the beautiful coastline around the cove, including the remarkable and superbly situated Minack Theatre, and craggy Logan Rock with Treryn Dinas Iron Age fort, perched high above the waves.

Just above the main car park can be found another of Porthcurno's surprises, the **Museum of Submarine Telegraphy**. Porthcurno was first used for communication purposes in the 1870s, from which time undersea cables were brought here from all over the world. For more than 90 years it was one of the most important centres for communication in the country. During World War II it played a vital role as a secret communications centre.

Leave the car park and walk left down the road, which climbs steeply uphill to reach the entrance to the Minack Theatre on the left.

A Turn left towards the theatre; the coast path is signed to the left of the entrance, and leads down steep, rugged steps round the edge of the theatre itself, with glorious views over the beach and clear water – on a hot sunny day you could be somewhere in the Mediterranean. The Minack Theatre is the result of one woman's inspiration and determination: Rowena Cade (1893–1983), who originated from Cheltenham, and who started

PUBLIC TRANSPORT None available
REFRESHMENTS Cable Station Inn, Porthcurno Hotel, Mariner's Lodge bar and restaurant, and café near Porthcurno beach; café and Logan Rock pub in Treen; coffee shop at Minack Theatre
PUBLIC TOILETS In the car park at Porthcurno near the car park at Treen
ORDNANCE SURVEY MAPS Explorer 102 (Land's End), Landranger 203 (Land's End & Isles of Scilly)

cutting out the theatre site by hand in 1932. This wonderful place now puts on a 17-week summer season of plays, come rain or shine. It has a visitor centre and museum, café and gift shop, and a superb display of sub-tropical plants.

? *When was the Eastern Telegraph Company formed?*

B Follow the path along the back of the beach to cross the track leading to the car park, and ahead up the other side of the beach to reach the pillbox. At the next junction of paths, keep right to reach a white pyramid, marking the site of the wooden hut that housed the end of the submarine telegraph cable laid from Brest in 1880. Follow the narrow path along the cliff edge as it runs behind Treen Cove to rejoin the coast path.

C Turn right onto Treen Cliff; ignore the bridlepath leading left, and keep straight on along the coast path. Just past another path to the left, and an NT contributions cairn, turn right to walk out onto the headland to have a look at the Logan Rock. This is also the site of Treryn Dinas, an Iron Age cliff castle, perched high above the weathered granite cliffs. The *Granite State* was wrecked off the Logan Rock in 1898.

A logan stone is a rocking stone, and the **Logan Rock** here is famous for being dislodged from its position in 1824 by naval **Lieutenant Goldsmith** and his friends, causing a public outcry. He was ordered to replace it by the Admiralty at his own expense, a complicated procedure considering the granite rock weighs more than 60 tons. It can still be rocked, but not as easily as in Lieutenant Goldsmith's time. Guides to the Logan Rock used to pick sea pinks from the cliffs for sale, and so became known as 'pinkers'.

D Retrace your steps to the cairn, and go straight ahead inland through the fields. Cross over two Cornish stiles, then over stone steps across the next hedgebank, and through a gap in the next bank. The path ends at a kissing gate; turn left along the rough track towards Treen. Where the track bends left, go straight ahead over granite steps to meet the lane by Larks Cottage; the Logan café and stores are right, with the car park and toilets. The Logan Inn will be found straight down the lane, and it has a great collection of old black-and-white photographs that detail the escapades of Lieutenant Goldsmith.

Retrace your steps from the pub to the café, turn right up the gritty bridlepath opposite. Where it veers sharp left, go straight ahead to enter the popular Treen Farm campsite. Make for the middle of the hedge that runs along the left side of the field, and leave over a stile with a footpath post and arrow. Walk diagonally across the next field to cross a stone stile in the corner. Follow the footpath post across the next field, and over a stone stile, and across the next field towards a metal gate and footpath post. Over a stone stile, and across the next field towards a metal gate, keeping the hedge on the right. Leave the field over a stone stile onto a narrow, hedged path that runs downhill. After 20 yds the coast path is met at a T-junction; turn right and keep straight ahead downhill to meet a track. Turn right into the car park. ●

Porthcurno beach, looking towards Logan Rock

15 *St Anthony-in-Meneague*

START Manaccan
DISTANCE 4¼ miles (6.8km)
TIME 2 hours
PARKING In the centre of Manaccan village, near the restored well
ROUTE FEATURES Fairly steep walk up lanes to leave Manaccan; some paths muddy after rain; dogs to be kept under control through Bosahan Estate.

Starting (or ending) at the characterful New Inn in peaceful Manaccan village, the route follows the edge of Helford River, with views across to the gardens at Trebah and Glendurgan, then runs around the end of Dennis Head to tucked-away St Anthony-in Meneague, with its beautiful church. This walk can easily be done in either direction

The sheltered **Helford River** is blessed with two beautiful gardens, both of which are open to the public: Glendurgan, dating from the early 19th century and now in the hands of the National Trust, and Trebah, which is privately owned. Both contain many rare and exotic plants, and are known for their collections of camellias, rhododendrons and azaleas, all of which flourish in the mild climate. Glendurgan also has a spectacular laurel maze.

Walk up the lane towards Helford, passing the school and children's playground, to the cross-roads. Walk straight over, and follow the quiet lane up and then downhill towards Helford.

> **When was the well in the centre of Manaccan restored, and why?**

A Where the lane bends sharp left, turn right down a narrow dead end lane signed Treath. Where that lane bends sharp left, turn right down the permissive path through the Bosahan estate. Look across the Helford River towards the Ferry

PUBLIC TRANSPORT Bus service from Truro via Helston
REFRESHMENTS The New Inn, Manaccan; shop selling ice-cream at St Anthony-in-Meneague
PUBLIC TOILETS None on route
CHILDREN'S PLAY AREA In Manaccan
ORDNANCE SURVEY MAPS Explorer 103 (The Lizard), Landranger 204 (Truro & Falmouth)

Boat Inn at Helford Passage. There has been a passenger ferry here since medieval times (when it belonged to the Bishops of Exeter). Until the early years of the 20th century, horses and carts were also carried over, the horses having to swim beside the ferry. Helford village itself, a popular yet exclusive holiday venue, was for many years an important port, exporting tin and copper, as evidenced by the fact that the village had its own custom house.

The path leads past Kennel Cottages and into woodland, thick with snowdrops in February and bluebells in May. Look across the river to the pretty little hamlet of Durgan, and the gardens at Glendurgan and Trebah.

B The path runs behind the privately owned Bosahan Cove, and onto sandy Ponsence Cove, popular with visitors who arrive by boat. Follow the coast path through woodland to emerge into fields via a kissing gate; look north-east for views of St Mawes and St Anthony lighthouse. Walk left along the bottom of the field, over a stone slab stile, and along the next field. Cross over a narrow stile, and along the bottom of the next field, which is left via a metal kissing gate. Walk up the next field, keeping the hedge left, with views over Gillan Creek to the right. The path leads into a gorsey area; turn left over a wooden stile (coast path signs). Take the second path left to wind around the end of Dennis Head. 'Dennis' derives from the Cornish 'dinas' (castle), and Iron Age earthworks here provide early evidence of the head's defensive position. The headland was fortified again during the Spanish Armada and Napoleonic wars, and was held by Royalists to protect the tin trade during the Civil War.

C Continue around the head to reach the wooden stile again. Turn right; at the next footpath post go left along the hedge, then walk diagonally down the field, which is left via a metal kissing gate onto a lane. Turn left, then right to pass the church via the churchyard. Rejoin the lane and turn right, to walk inland up Gillan Creek, which can be crossed on foot at low tide. Follow the lane to the T-junction just beyond the end of the creek at Carne.

D Turn right along the lane signed for Manaccan. A little way up, turn right to cross the stream on a marked footpath; the steep, wooded path leads to a stone stile, then levels off to run through deep

The original Norman church of **St Anthony-in Meneague** (meaning 'the land of the monks' in Cornish – there were ancient ecclesiastical establishments locally at Manaccan and St Keverne) is set in an idyllic yet very isolated position on the edge of Gillan Creek. Extended in the 15th century, legend has it that it was built by a group of grateful shipwrecked Normans, saved after being storm-driven to Cornwall from France. The legend is supported by the fact that the tower is built of a fine-grained granite found nowhere else in Cornwall, but found in Normandy. Other suggestions are that the church was built to commemorate the landing place of a Celtic saint.

banks, and over a granite stile into a field. Follow the path left, and over a stone slab stile at the top of the field; then over another and down a deeply-banked lane to meet a rough lane. Turn left; at the end of the lane go straight across to enter the churchyard. Look out for the old fig tree that grows out of the church wall; it is said that anyone picking figs will experience bad luck and that the whole village will suffer should the tree be damaged. Leave the churchyard via a metal gate and turn left, then right by the post office and down a narrow path to the centre of the village and your car. ●

The view across Helford Passage

Veryan and Portloe

START Veryan
DISTANCE 3½ miles (5.6km)
TIME 1¾ hours
PARKING On the side of the road near the parish hall in the centre of Veryan
ROUTE FEATURES Steep climb up the lane out of Portloe

16

Veryan is perhaps best known for its five roundhouses, seen on so many picture postcards. But just a mile or so away lies the coast and the old fishing village of Portloe, which makes an excellent focus for an easy walk through rolling farmland and quiet lanes – and there's even a pub at each end.

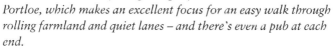 Cross the road from the parish hall to the footpath by the ornamental gardens, signed 'To Portloe via Trewartha'. Walk through the wooden gate and along the path, with the church above right. The path leads through a kissing gate into the playground. Walk to the top right corner, cross the stream and into the field over a Cornish stile. Cross the field diagonally, keeping to the right of two big lime trees.

A Turn right over a stile between granite posts to enter a narrow strip of woodland. Leave the

woodland over a stile, then straight over the field, keeping the trees. Leave the field over a stile in the top right corner, onto Century Lane.

Veryan's pretty church of **St Symphorian** (a French saint dating from the 10th century), largely rebuilt in 1847, is well worth investigation. In the churchyard can be found what is reputed to be the longest grave in Britain, holding the crew of the German barque *Hera*. She was wrecked on the Gull Rock in 1914, and the crew of 19 were buried in one long grave, paid for by the parish.

PUBLIC TRANSPORT Bus service from St Austell and Truro
REFRESHMENTS New Inn in Veryan; Ship Inn, Lugger Hotel, and Tregain restaurant and tearoom in Portloe
PUBLIC TOILETS In the centre of Veryan; in Portloe
ORDNANCE SURVEY MAPS Explorer 105 (Falmouth & Mevagissey), Landranger 204 (Truro & Falmouth)

B Turn left. At the crossroads go straight ahead, signed Portloe. Pass Camels House on the left, with its unusual 'decorated' wall; look out for glimpses of the sea ahead. Where the lane bends sharp left, go through the gates to Broom é Parc across the road on the right; Broom é Parc was used in the filming of the TV adaptation of Mary Wesley's *The Camomile Lawn*. Ignore the path leading off left, and go straight ahead on a National Trust footpath. The gritty

path runs between the house and the walled garden, to reach the coast path.

C Turn sharp left and follow the path below the garden, edged with hydrangeas. Go up a steep flight of stone steps and over a hedgebank, then over a wooden stile into a field; look back for lovely views over Parc Caragloose Cove, and Nare Head and Gull Rock beyond. Continue along the coast path, and over a stile to reach a gorsey area above Manare Point, with views ahead to Dodman Point. Follow the coast path downhill towards the pretty, unspoilt fishing village of Portloe, situated at the mouth of a narrow valley. The path leads around the edge of the jagged igneous outcrop of rock known as

The building of Veryan's famous **roundhouses** was initiated by the rector, and they were constructed by a builder from Lostwithiel around 1820. Each one is adorned with a cross, and the idea behind their shape is that the Devil would be unable to hide in a house with no corners. There is a pair of these pretty little buildings, with Gothic revival windows, at each end of the village, and one in the centre. Veryan also has two holy wells.

The Jacka (watch out for areas of unfenced cliff), then turns inland to reach the slipway, with public toilets on the left. Portloe's little harbour was partly responsible for the fact that during the 17 years that a lifeboat was stationed here it never once saw action: in rough weather it was impossible to negotiate the narrow entrance.

D From the slipway turn left steeply uphill to pass the church on the right and the tearoom on the left. Go straight on uphill, away from the sea, passing the Ship Inn on the right. When Sunny Corner is reached, and the lane bends left, turn right over the stream, signed public footpath to Veryan. Follow the tarmac path to the left to pass the Old Cottage on the left on a grassy area, and through a small metal gate into a field. Walk along the bottom edge; where the hedge veers left, walk straight across and up the field to steep granite steps over the hedgebank, and into the next field. Turn left, keeping the hedgebank on the left. Go through the left of the two large metal gates at the top of the field and onto a track between high banks, and on through Trewartha Hall farm buildings.

At the entrance to the farm, turn right along the lane, which runs

View across Portloe harbour

through the hamlet of Trewartha to reach the road.

E Turn left, then, almost immediately, right on a tarmac lane, signed Veryan, to pass the converted Trewartha Chapel. The lane ends at a gate into a field; walk straight across the field and through a narrow strip of woodland via two hedgebanks and a gate. Walk downhill to pass the two big lime trees, left into the playground, and retrace your steps to your car. ●

? *Who was responsible for erecting the well in Veryan, which you can find near the public toilets?*

17 *Lamorna and Mousehole*

START Lamorna Cove
DISTANCE 5¼ miles (8.4km)
TIME 2½ hours
PARKING Car park (fee-paying) at the quay at Lamorna Cove
ROUTE FEATURES Rocky coast path, steeply undulating in places; steep descent/ascent to/from Mousehole along lane

A popular yet peaceful route along the undulating coast path from secluded Lamorna Cove to the quintessential Cornish fishing village of Mousehole, with its sheltered harbour and narrow, flower-filled alleyways and courts, perfect for a relaxing exploration on foot. This walk can easily be done in either direction; there is a clearly signed fee-paying car park in Mousehole.

From the quay, walk a few steps inland, then turn right to walk in front of the row of cottages, with their gardens between the path and the sea. Cross the stream (public toilets to the left) and follow the unsigned rocky coast path past the granite quarry on the left, and walk on to the craggy headland at Carn-du, pink with sea thrift in May, from where there are superb views back to the cove.

A The path continues down rough granite steps to run along

Tragically, the village of **Mousehole** hit the headlines just before Christmas in 1981 when the entire crew of the Penlee lifeboat – *Solomon Browne* – was lost while attempting to save the crew of the cargo vessel the *Union Star*, which was wrecked below Boscawen Point to west of Lamorna Cove. This sad event is commemorated by a garden at the lifeboat house, and by a memorial at the church of St Paul de Leon at Paul, on the way to Newlyn.

the level low-lying Kemyel Cliff, then passes into Kemyel Crease Nature Reserve, owned by the Cornwall Wildlife Trust since

---

PUBLIC TRANSPORT None available
REFRESHMENTS Lamorna Wink pub and café at Lamorna Cove, Ship Inn and cafés at Mousehole
PUBLIC TOILETS At Lamorna Cove; by the harbour in Mousehole
ORDNANCE SURVEY MAPS Explorer 102 (Land's End), Landranger 203 (Land's End & Isles of Scilly)

1974, and a haven for insects, butterflies and birds. This sheltered, frost-free part of the Cornish coast, between here and Mousehole, has long been terraced for the cultivation of bulbs. Daffodils were grown for the London markets, and potatoes were cultivated here during World War II. As a result, much of the existing vegetation has a 'civilised' feel, with Monterey pines (unique to this part of the coast, and so a familiar landmark for passing vessels), fuchsias and hydrangeas. The next part of the coast path, as far as the disused coastguard lookout on Penzer Point, is extremely undulating, with many stepped ascents and descents. Eventually, the path levels and runs

There are a number of theories as to how the old pilchard-fishing village of **Mousehole** – pronounced 'Mouzel' locally – got its name. The village's original Cornish name is Porth Enys ('the landing place of the island'), after St Clement's island lying just offshore, which in turn is named after a hermit who used to live there. Many believe that its name was taken from **The Mousehole cave**, just north of Cape Spaniard; others think that Mousehole derives from the Cornish words 'mouz hel', meaning 'maiden's brook'. This part of the coast has long been associated with smuggling: the **Lamorna Wink** is so-named because of the local practice of turning a blind eye to what was going on.

a little inland to meet a gritty track. Asphodel House, on the right, overlooks Point Spaniard, where

Mousehole harbour in the summer

B Turn right; follow the lane steeply down into Mousehole. Just past the huge Wesleyan church on the left, turn right to have a look at the harbour (public toilets right).

It's not hard to understand why Mousehole is popular with artists, and why it was a favourite subject for the 19th-century Newlyn School of Artists, whose work can be seen at the Newlyn Art Gallery in Penzance. The Ship Inn overlooks the harbour.

the Spaniards landed in 1595 before destroying Mousehole, Paul, Newlyn and Penzance. It is said that only one building in Mousehole survived: the Keigwin Arms, now a private house, but restored in Elizabethan manor house style.

? *When was the Wesleyan church in Mousehole built?*

C Retrace your steps back up the steep hill, passing the Wild Bird Hospital and Sanctuary (admission free) on the right. Walk past the coast path and keep uphill on the lane to reach the hamlet at

Raginnis. Where a footpath sign on the corner directs you right through Raginnis, turn left over the Cornish stile into the field. Walk straight across the field, and over the stile; walk along the top of the next field, keeping the hedgebank on the right. Cross the next two stiles, keeping to the top of the next two fields. Cross a stile into the next field, and keep the hedgebank on the right; at the top corner leave over a stone stile to reach Kemyel Drea.

Mousehole, much-loved by artists

D Go through the gate at the edge of the farmyard and straight ahead over four stiles on a narrow path between the farm buildings. Follow the footpath sign left, then right across a grassy area to join a signed path which veers right between high hedgebanks. The path runs through a boggy area on stone slabs, over a stile, then over another into a field. Keeping the hedge on the right, leave at the top of the field over a stone stile and turn left onto the lane, opposite Kemyel House. Walk along the lane through Kemyel Crease farm.

E Follow the footpath sign up the bank and over the hedge into a field, and make for the footpath post in the far right corner. From there, make for a stone stile over the next bank, then cross a Cornish stile, and walk towards Kemyel Wartha, keeping the hedgebank right. When you reach the track by the buildings, follow footpath signs left. The track passes to the left of some converted farm buildings; where the track bends right keep straight ahead on a grassy track. Where the path is signed both ahead and left, turn left between high hedges. As the top of Lamorna Cove is reached, follow footpath posts past the quarry on the left and drop downhill to rejoin the coast path. Turn right to cross the stream, then left for your car. ●

18 *Port Quin to Port Isaac*

START Port Quin

DISTANCE 5 miles (8km)

TIME 3 hours

PARKING National Trust car park at Port Quin (contributions cairn)

ROUTE FEATURES Dogs to be kept on leads through farmland from Port Quin to Port Isaac; very strenuous coast path, with many steps and steep ascents and descents

Port Quin and Port Isaac are two of Cornwall's gems: the walk starts from the old pilchard-fishing hamlet of Port Quin, now in the hands of the National Trust, and leads to peaceful Port Isaac, one of the north coast's few reasonable natural harbours, before returning along a particularly beautiful yet tough stretch of the coastal footpath. Not a walk for the faint-hearted.

Walk out of the car park and turn right uphill away from the sea.

A About 50 yds up the lane turn left, following footpath signs for Port Isaac, to pass in front of Howard's Cottage. Go over a Cornish stile by a white gate and into the field. Walk up the valley (boggy in winter), and through two hedgebanks; the path then veers uphill and left. At the top of the field pass over a Cornish stile between two five-bar gates. Walk along the track through large, sweeping arable fields: any sense of being anywhere near the sea is soon left far behind. Pass over the next two stiles, keeping on the

The hamlet of **Port Quin** lies on a small natural harbour. There are disused antimony mines to the west, above Gibson's Cove. Mining supplemented the income gained from pilchard pressing and salting which took place in the old buildings behind the rocky cove, many of which have now been converted into holiday accommodation by the National Trust. Some know Port Quin as 'the village that died': legend has it that every local man perished in one shipwreck in the 19th century.

PUBLIC TRANSPORT None available

REFRESHMENTS Golden Lion pub, Old School, Slipway Hotel, Harbour café and restaurant at Port Isaac; picnic tables at Port Quin

PUBLIC TOILETS In Port Isaac

ORDNANCE SURVEY MAPS Explorer 106 (Newquay & Padstow), Landranger 200 (Newquay & Bodmin)

track; look left for views of Tintagel along the coast. Cross over another stile just level with Roscarrock farm.

B The track bends sharp right towards the farm; turn left (unsigned) and keep along the edge of the field to the bottom; follow the hedgebank right, and turn left over a wooden stile; look left for views of Pine Haven. The narrow path winds steeply downhill to reach the bottom of the combe. Turn left over a wooden railed footbridge, then over a big Cornish stile (ignoring the path to Pine Haven to the left) and steeply uphill through brambles and gorse and out of the combe. The path leads into a field; keep straight ahead, passing to the left of a post on the hill ahead. Walk straight ahead and over a Cornish stile, with views of Port Isaac directly

Peaceful Port Quin

Cornish stile above Port Isaac

tend to use the car park at the top of the hill and walk in. Those who do park on the beach below the Platt at low tide always run the risk of getting the time wrong and returning to their car just that little bit too late.

D Having explored the village and prepared yourself for the return route, retrace your steps to the top of Roscarrock Hill, with perfect views over the harbour. Keep on the coast path as it runs in front of the last houses on the left, and up steps onto the open cliff. The path levels as it passes through a gap in a hedgebank, then runs round the edge of Lobber Point. Views of Port Isaac are quickly lost, emphasising its incredibly sheltered position. The path

ahead. Pick your way down the edge of the next field, keeping the hedge on the left. The path leads over a slate slab and down steps to emerge on a gritty track (the coast path) at the top of Roscarrock Hill.

C Turn right and walk steeply downhill into the centre of Port Isaac, passing the toilets on the left at the bottom of the hill, and the pottery and gallery in the old chapel on the right. One of Port Isaac's major advantages is that the narrow, twisty streets make parking almost impossible, and visitors

then drops down to pretty Pine Cove, and over a wooden stile, signed Port Quin. Cross the stream via a wooden bridge, then climb two long flights of steps up the other side of the combe. Follow the path to reach Varley Head, and over a stile across the neck of the head; then over another stile behind Greengarden Cove. *Note: much of this stretch of the coast path is unfenced, and caution should be exercised at all times.*

? *How many steps are there in the two flights ascending after leaving Pine Cove on the coast path?*

From here, the switchback coast path can be seen running all the way along to Kellan Head, and this is where the hard work really begins, with many steep ascents and descents, and a horrible number of steps – but it is worth it. Once Kellan Head is reached, there are lovely views of Doyden Castle on Doyden Point ahead: this folly, now in the care of the National Trust and available as holiday accommodation, was built soon after Samuel Symmons bought the headland in 1827, so that he could provide a suitable venue for a bit of out-of-the-way drinking and gambling with his colleagues.

E From Kellan Head follow the coast path as it runs inland (with several more flights of steps) to reach the top of the slipway at Port Quin; note the drinking-water tap on the wall opposite, which you may well be in need of at this point. Turn left to regain the car park. ●

19 *St Anthony Head*

A long yet not strenuous walk which takes in some of the best features of the south Cornwall coast: great views across the River Fal to St Mawes with its 16th-century castle, and Falmouth beyond; stunning Place House and church of St Anthony-in-Roseland; the beautiful coast path to St Anthony Head, with its lighthouse and battery; and golden sandy beaches at Porthbeor and Porth.

START Porth Farm

DISTANCE 5½ miles (8.8km)

TIME 3 hours

PARKING Two National Trust car parks at Porth Farm (50p honesty box); park in the first one on the right

ROUTE FEATURES Narrow wooded path along Percuil River; some paths muddy after wet weather

From the car park entrance follow the footpath sign right along the edge of the car park field, signed Percuil River and Place Quay, to pass through a wooded area.

A The path turns left over a railed footbridge, through a gate and then right to run along the bottom of the field with Porth Creek on the right. Cross a wooden stile and follow this narrow, rooty path through mixed deciduous woodland as it veers left to run

The tip of the **Roseland Peninsula** ('ros' is Cornish for promontory), bounded by the Carrick Roads and River Fal on the west, and by Veryan Bay and Gerrans Bay on the east, has been a site of great strategic importance for hundreds of years, guarding the entrance to the great natural harbour of the Carrick Roads. Most of what can be seen at St Anthony Battery dates from the end of the 19th century, much now tastefully converted into holiday accommodation by the National Trust, which took over the site in 1959.

along the Percuil River, with views

PUBLIC TRANSPORT Bus service from St Austell, Truro and St Mawes to Portscatho only

REFRESHMENTS Royal Standard pub at Gerrans, Plume of Feathers pub in Portscatho, both north of Porth

PUBLIC TOILETS At St Anthony Head, and opposite Porth Farm

ORDNANCE SURVEY MAPS Explorer 105 (Falmouth & Mevagissey), Landranger 204 (Truro & Falmouth)

Map labels:
St Mawes · North-hill Point · Porth Creek · Froe · NTL · Boat Yard · Quay · Porth Farm · Towan · P 19 · 33 · Polvarth Point · Black Rock · Drawler Plantation · Bohortha · 86 · 87 · St Mawes Harbour · Amsterdam Point · Cellars Beach · SWC Path · Place · Roseland Place · SWC Path · 32 · Porthbeor Beach · Porthmellin Head · St Anthony · Place · Military Road · Drake's Downs · Zone Point · 31 · Anthony Head

0 · 1 KM · HALF MILE

Place House was built in 1840 on the site of an Elizabethan house, which itself replaced an earlier priory. The lovely little church of St Anthony-in-Roseland is joined to the house by the north transept, and has a superb Norman south door. The church is a rare survival in that it avoided the widespread restoration and rebuilding of many Cornish churches in the 15th century. There was probably a small church here in the mid-10th century, and the place does have a wonderfully ancient feel.

across to St Mawes, a popular sailing centre, and headquarters of the Roseland Gig Club (the club's oldest gig, the *Newquay*, was built in 1812) opposite. After a long wooded stretch, the path crosses a stile to enter a field, then crosses another stile back into woodland again. Views of Henry VIII's impressive 15th-century St Mawes Castle, with Falmouth beyond, open up to the right. Walk past St Mawes ferry point at Totty's Steps (at high water the ferry lands at Place Quay), through a kissing gate, through a meadow and then another kissing gate to gain the lane at Place Quay, with splendid Place House opposite.

B Turn left up the lane, with great views of the sweeping lawns in front of Place House on the right, formerly the site of a mill pond. About 100 yds up the lane turn right over a slate stile, following coast path signs to St Anthony Head. The path leads through the overgrown and atmospheric graveyard of the beautiful 12th/13th-century church of St Anthony-in-Roseland. Follow the path up stone steps from the south door of the church to pass an old orchard on the left, then right to join a broad track. Turn right and follow the track as it runs around the back of Place House and along Cellars Beach. The private cottages ahead were formerly pilchard cellars, where the catch was processed for export to the Catholic countries of Europe.

C Turn left over a wooden stile to leave the track, signed St Anthony Head, and walk up the field. Pass over a Cornish stile at the top, with fantastic views of St Mawes and Pendennis castles ahead. Walk straight on very steeply downhill, then turn left to walk along low cliffs. Leave the field over a stile and follow the coast path round Carricknath Point, then over a stile before dropping steeply down through a gate and over a wooden walkway at the back of Great Molunan beach, a great spot for picnics and rock-pooling. Follow the coast path right to pass through a white gate onto St Anthony Head (National Trust). Where the coast path bends sharp left and uphill, walk straight on to have a look at the lighthouse (now holiday accommodation), built in 1834 (though a beacon had been burnt here for many years before then) to warn mariners of the dangers of The Manacles reef and to watch over the entrance to the Carrick Roads. From 1882 a large bell (the largest in Cornwall) was rung in foggy conditions, replaced by a fog-horn in 1954. Retrace your steps and follow the coast path steeply uphill to reach the car park at St Anthony Battery.

D Turn right to walk past the converted officers' quarters; opposite Tiffy's take the tarmac path around the end of the point past the gun emplacements and toposcope, and above the World War II observation post. Rejoin the grassy coast path and pass through a gate and straight on across Drake's Downs, with views of Porthbeor beach ahead. This

> **?** *What was stored in the small white building to the right of the coast path just after Great Molunan beach?*

stretch of the coast is good for spotting fulmar and gannets. The path crosses two stiles before running along the back of Porthbeor beach and Elwinick Cove, then around Porthmellin and Killigerran Heads – the coastal grassland is particularly lovely here, ecologically managed and supporting a wide range of wildflowers – before descending to long, low-lying Towan beach (towan is Cornish for sand dune).

Note the wreck post on the right, erected by the coastguard service and used to simulate a ship's mast in training exercises. Turn left at the back of the beach and walk inland on an old sanding road, used in the past to transport seaweed from the beach by donkey and packhorse, for use as fertiliser. The path passes through a National Trust building housing toilets, to reach the road opposite Porth Farm. ●

Place House

20 *Trevone and Stepper Point*

The section of coast between Trevone and Stepper Point is characterised by dramatic, tortured slate cliffs and wide-ranging views towards Pentire Point. But this is a walk of contrasts: the second part, turning inland along the edge of the broad sweep of the Camel estuary, feels calm and safe by comparison, as does the return to Trevone across rolling arable farmland hamlet of Crugmeer.

START Trevone Bay

DISTANCE 5 miles (8km)

TIME 2½ hours

PARKING Car park (fee-paying in summer)) at the beach at Trevone

ROUTE FEATURES Many high Cornish stiles; take care on all sections of the coast path from Trevone to Stepper Point; unfenced and precipitous for much of the route; beware the Round Hole at Trevone

Leave the car park through the entrance and turn right.

> **?** *How large an area does the Stepper Point access area cover?*

A Follow coast path signs up concrete steps onto the open cliff, and walk around the end of Round Hole Point. The Round Hole itself, a collapsed sea cave, lies a little inland up the cliff. There is a huge contrast here between the view over the sandy beach at Trevone, to the south-west, and the magnificent, unforgiving, indented coastline ahead. The path runs along a broad, level, grassy section of cliff to pass an unusual area of limestone cliff at Marble Cliff, Porthmissen: most of the north Cornwall coast is composed of slate, with headlands formed of resistant igneous rock. The path runs along the back of Longcarrow Cove, then over a Cornish stile, before dropping steeply down and veering inland to cross a small combe on a wooden footbridge.

PUBLIC TRANSPORT Bus service from Bodmin, Newquay, Truro and Wadebridge

REFRESHMENTS Rocky Point beach café at Trevone beach; Well Parc pub in Trevone; also café at Prideaux Place (afternoons Sunday–Thursday)

PUBLIC TOILETS At Trevone beach

ORDNANCE SURVEY MAPS Explorer 106 Newquay & Padstow, Landranger 200 (Newquay & Bodmin)

small combe. Follow footpath posts left and then right straight up the cliff (this is very steep) to meet the next footpath post at the top overlooking the detached sections of cliff that have formed the extraordinarily contorted Lower, Middle and Higher Merope islands. *Note: extreme care should be taken here.*

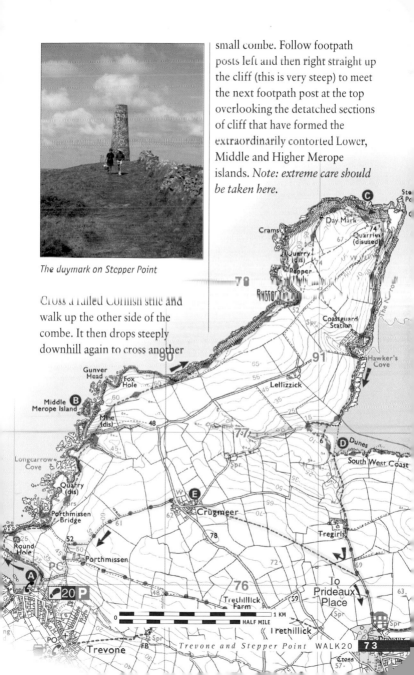

The daymark on Stepper Point

Cross a railed Cornish stile and walk up the other side of the combe. It then drops steeply downhill again to cross another

B Follow the coast path right as it levels out and runs along the cliffs towards Butter Hole, crossing a Cornish stile en route. Look out for fulmar, razorbill and guillemot offshore. The path drops down to pass through a kissing gate to enter the Stepper Point access area. Stepper Point is composed of greenstone, and, in the past, has been heavily quarried for roadstone. Cross the next stile, then reach a kissing gate at the back of Butter Hole: look out for the fantastic green and purple bands of slate in the cliff-face here. Follow the path around the back of the cove, and footpath posts onto Stepper Point to reach the Pepperpot, a daymark constructed in 1832 by the Association for the Preservation of Life and Property. There are wonderful views from here up the expansive Camel estuary, and across Padstow Bay to Polzeath and beyond.

C From the daymark, follow the coast path downhill; ignore the path right to the coastguard lookout. The next footpath post directs you right through the broken-down hedgebank near St John's Well.

Leave Stepper Point over a stile and walk inland, with superb views over Daymer Bay and Brae Hill, where on summer evenings you can listen to readings of Sir John Betjeman's poetry. He is buried at St Enodoc Church, which can be spotted peeping out from the sand

Sandy Harbour Cove, with Hawker's Cove beyond

dunes just to the left of Brae Hill. Walk through the next kissing gate; the path becomes narrow and gritty (wonderful blackberries in September), to reach Hawker's Cove via another kissing gate. The older property here was built in 1847 to house the pilots who helped vessels negotiate the notorious and potentially lethal Doom Bar, a shifting sandbank across the estuary responsible for more than 300 shipwrecks from 1760 to 1920; the other cottages were built for coastguards.

Follow coast path signs around the back of the cove past the slipway, to rejoin the lane and turn left, and over a wooden stile to continue on a gritty path past the old lifeboat station, built in 1827. Shifting sands rendered it unusable, and in 1967 the Padstow lifeboat moved west to Mother Ivey's Bay. Continue over a Cornish stile to reach the back of Sandy Harbour Cove, where boats were moored until the 1920s when the main navigation channel down the estuary moved out of reach.

The path runs inland to cross a track and over a wooden footbridge. Go over the next stile and left along the edge of the field; over the next stile, over a wooden footbridge and on to a track; turn right.

Prideaux Place was built by the Prideaux family in the 16th century and is now occupied by their descendants. Surrounded by beautiful gardens, mainly laid out in Georgian and Victorian times, the estate also boasts a deer park dating from 1750; legend has it that if the deer were ever to die out that would herald the end of the Prideaux family. A tunnel leads from the grounds to the 13th/14th-century St Petroc's Church, giving the family private access to Padstow's main place of worship.

D Where the coast path is signed left, go straight ahead uphill on a gritty track (unsigned); at the top of the track turn right to reach Tregirls Farm. Turn left down the drive, which soon becomes tarmac; follow the lane over the brow of the hill (for Prideaux Place keep straight on). Turn right over a stile and walk diagonally right across the field. Cross the farm track and go over the stile, and diagonally left across the next field. Over the next two stiles, and diagonally left across the next field, and over four more stiles to reach a track on the edge of Crugmeer.

E Turn left; at the T-junction turn right, and immediately left down a gritty lane which eventually runs downhill past Porthmissen to reach the car park at Trevone. ●

Further Information

Walking Safety

The walks in this book cover a varied range of landscapes. Whereas most are set in reasonably gentle countryside that offers no real dangers to walkers at any time of year, extra care should always be exercised on any route that follows sections of the South West Coast Path. Wherever you walk, it is still advisable to take sensibe walking precautions and follow certain well-tried guidelines.

Always take with you both warm and waterproof clothing and sufficient food and drink. Wear suitable footwear, i.e. strong walking boots or shoes that give a good grip over stony ground, on slippery slopes and in muddy conditions. Try to obtain a local weather forecast and bear it in mind before you start. Do not be afraid to abandon your proposed route and return to your starting point in the event of a sudden and unexpected deterioration in the weather.

All the walks described in this book will be safe to do, given due care

Port Isaac from the coast path

and respect, even during the winter. Indeed, a crisp, fine winter day often provides perfect walking conditions, with firm ground underfoot and a clarity unique to this time of the year.

The most difficult hazard likely to be encountered is mud, especially when walking along woodland and field paths, farm tracks and bridleways – the latter in particular can often get churned up by cyclists and horses. In summer, an additional difficulty may be narrow and overgrown paths, particularly along the edges of cultivated fields. Neither should constitute a major problem provided that the appropriate footwear is worn.

Follow the Country Code
- Enjoy the countryside and respect its life and work
- Guard against all risk of fire
- Take your litter home
- Fasten all gates
- Help to keep all water clean
- Keep your dogs under control
- Protect wildlife, plants and trees
- Keep to public paths across farmland
- Take special care on country roads
- Leave livestock, crops and machinery alone
- Make no unnecessary noise
- Use gates and stiles to cross fences, hedges and walls
  (The Countryside Agency)

Useful organisations

Council for the Protection of Rural England
Warwick House,
25 Buckingham Palace Road,
London
SW1W 0PP.
Tel. 020 7976 6433;
Fax 020 7976 6373
E-mail: cpre@gn.apc.org

Countryside Agency
John Dower House,
Crescent Place,
Cheltenham
GL50 3RA.
Tel. 01242 521381;
Fax 01242 584270
www.countryside.gov.uk

English Heritage
23 Savile Row, London W1X 1AB.
Tel. 020 7973 3434;
Fax 020 7973 3001
www.english-heritage.org.uk

English Nature
Northminster House,
Peterborough, Cambridgeshire
PE1 1UA.
Tel. 01733 455100;
Fax 01733 455103
Website: www.english-nature.org.uk

National Trust
Membership and general enquiries
PO Box 39, Bromley,
Kent BR1 3XL.
Tel. 0181 315 1111

Cornwall Regional Office
Lanhydrock, Bodmin, PL30 4DE.
Tel. 01208 74281

Ordnance Survey
Romsey Road, Maybush,
Southampton SO16 4GU.
Tel. 08456 05 05 05 (Lo-call)
Website: www.ordsvy.gov.uk

Public Transport:
For all public transport enquiries in
South-West England
Tel. 0870 6082608

Ramblers' Association
2nd Floor, Camelford House,
87–90 Albert Embankment,
London SE1 7TW.
Tel. 020 7339 8585;
Fax 020 7339 8501
www.ramblers.org.uk

Royal Society for the Protection of Birds (RSPB)
The Lodge, Sandy, Beds
SG19 2DL.
Tel. 01767 680551;
Fax 01767 692365
www.rspb.org.uk

Cornwall Tourist Board
Pydar House, Pydar, St Truro
TR1 1EA
Tel. 01872 322900
Local tourist information offices
Bude: 01288 354240
Camelford: 01840 212954
Falmouth: 01326 312300
Fowey: 01726 833616
Helston & Lizard Peninsula:
01326 565431
Launceston: 01566 772321
Looe: 01503 262072
Newquay: 01637 854020
Padstow: 01841 533449
Penzance: 01736 362207
Plymouth: 01752 266030

Wooden sculpture at Cotehele

St Ives: 01736 796297
Isles of Scilly: 01720 422536
Truro: 01872 274555

Youth Hostels Association
Trevelyan House,
Dimple Road, Matlock,
Derbyshire DE4 3YH
Tel. 01629 592600
Website: www.yha.org.uk

Ordnance Survey Maps of Cornwall
Explorer maps 102 (Land's End, Penzance & St Ives), 103 (The Lizard, Falmouth & Helston), 104 (Redruth & St Agnes), 105 (Falmouth & Mevagissey) 106 (Newquay & Padstow),107 (St Austell & Liskeard), 108 (Lower Tamar Valley & Plymouth), 111 (Bude, Boscastle & Tintagel), 112 (Launceston & Holsworthy), and 126 (Clovelly & Hartland) Landranger maps 190 (Bude & Clovelly), 200 (Newquay & Bodmin), 201 (Plymouth & Launceston), 203 (Land's End & Isles of Scilly) and 204 (Truro & Falmouth).

Answers to Questions
Walk 1: A very large rabbit, which lives in a hutch by the front door – a sign at the pottery reads 'To buy a pot, ring the bell, or call in at Wood

Gorse and heather at Wheal Coates

Cottage next-door-but-one where the rabbit lives'.

Walk 2: The company helped in the restoration of the estate's woodlands after the great storm of January 1990 (the seat is passed on the way to Garden Cottage).

Walk 3: He drowned while bathing near Land's End on Saturday 19 May, 1894.

Walk 4: 620ft (189m) (information available at the trig point on top of the beacon).

Walk 5: By G. James Allday in 1951 (information available on a plaque just before the gate leading into Covington Wood).

Walk 6: It is the holy well of St Ia and, until 1843, formed the main water supply for Downalong (this part of St Ives).

Walk 7: In 1896, 'by public subscription for the use and enjoyment of the nation' (information available on a plaque to the right of the coast path on the way to Barras Nose).

Walk 8: Every 20 minutes.

Walk 9: Between 10.00 and 18.30; the warning is given by the flying of red flags, and a continuous blast on the hooter (information available on a notice at the edge of the quarry).

Walk 10: White Gate cottage.

Walk 11: The *Anna Maria* in 1859, rescuing 17 people.

Walk 12: Edna's; placed there by Ronald, Gillian and Richard (inscription on the kissing gate just before the path leading to Hawker's Hut).

Walk 13: *The Northern Belle*.

Walk 14: In 1870 (details on a plaque on the white pyramid seen during point B of the walk).

Walk 15: In 1977, for Queen Elizabeth II's Silver Jubilee.

Walk 16: Rev Samuel J.P. Trist; it was restored in 1912 to commemorate the coronation of King George V and Queen Mary.

Walk 17: 1905.

Walk 18: $148 + 29 = 178$.

Walk 19: Paraffin; this is where paraffin for the lighthouse at St Anthony Head used to be kept.

Walk 20: A total of 138 acres (56 ha) – information available on a noticeboard at the entrance to the access area.